W9-CHB-849

LEARNING AND TEACHING
THROUGH THE SENSES

Books by *Kathrene McLandress Tobey*

Published by THE WESTMINSTER PRESS

Learning and Teaching Through the Senses
The Church Plans for Kindergarten Children

Learning and Teaching Through the Senses

by Kathrene McLandress Tobey

THE WESTMINSTER PRESS / Philadelphia

PHILLIPS MEMORIAL
LIBRARY
PROVIDENCE COLLEGE

LB
1067
T6

COPYRIGHT © MCMLXX THE WESTMINSTER PRESS

All rights reserved—no part of this book may be reproduced in any form without permission in writing from the publisher, except by a reviewer who wishes to quote brief passages in connection with a review in magazine or newspaper.

Scripture quotations from the Revised Standard Version of the Bible are copyright, 1946 and 1952, by the Division of Christian Education of the National Council of Churches, and are used by permission.

STANDARD BOOK NO. 664-24874-8

LIBRARY OF CONGRESS CATALOG CARD NO. 70-92899

PHOTO CREDITS

Bayer of Monkmeyer: p. 106; COEMAR: p. 30; Sam L. Coplin: p. 56; Fred De Wys: front cover, p. 96; Djoma: p. 98; Virgil E. Foster: pp. 45, 47, 53, 61, 63, 87, 112, 121; Hays of Monkmeyer: p. 39; Samuel W. Hersch: p. 15; Fran Kelsey: p. 37; A. Alexander Nesbitt; pp. 8, 79, back cover; James G. Saint, Jr.: p. 103; Jackson Schutte: pp. 19, 117; Dr. M. P. Testa: p. 83; Kathrene McLandress Tobey, pp. 69, 109; Joe Tritsch: p. 25; Webster Institute of Math, Science, and the Arts: p. 54.

BOOK DESIGN
BY PATRICIA PENNINGTON

PUBLISHED BY THE WESTMINSTER PRESS ®
PHILADELPHIA, PENNSYLVANIA

PRINTED IN THE UNITED STATES OF AMERICA

With Appreciation to

My Parents—
   first teachers of perceptual learnings

Hamlin—
   partner in continual learning and teaching

Contents

Foreword

In this time of rapid change and rebellion against tradition, church education is being constantly reexamined for its relevancy to life. Technologists believe that the next decade will bring more change at a faster pace than that which we have already experienced. This means that adults are being forced to acknowledge, accept, and live with change.

"The church is dead, long live the church" is a current phrase that indicates disenchantment with the established patterns and dedication to the power of the living community of faith in Jesus Christ. For the sake of this faith the church is in the process of revamping its educational resources, of discovering new objectives, of adventuring in various ways of learning.

Educators in recent years have laid stress on the need for perceptual experiences that will stimulate intellectual growth. Such sensory experiences involve a learner directly: it is he who does the touching, seeing, or tasting, not the teacher. As he becomes involved he learns. The more senses he uses the better he learns. As he expresses himself in the arts and languages, he clarifies and retains learning. Perceptual experiences are basic for building concepts and living a satisfying life with oneself, in relation to God, others, and the world.

This book is about teachers and leaders who deliberately use the senses to heighten perceptual learning. They recognize themselves as learners, too, in the community of faith that is composed of all age groups. I appreciate their willingness to let me report experiences that might be suggestive to other leaders. The writer's own experience is also used and no doubt colors the way in which the experiences of others are interpreted. Some of the material here originally appeared in the *International Journal of Religious Education,* whose editor suggested it be enlarged for a book. In sharing these teaching-learning situations with you it is my hope that you too may venture into different experiences for more effective learning and teaching.

K.M.T.

New York City

1
Why Learn Through the Senses?

From northern Europe comes the custom of using Advent wreaths during the month of December to prepare family members for the coming of the Christ-child as they think of him in worship. It is an evergreen wreath with four candles on it to be used at family worship time. One candle is lighted the first week and another lighted each week to indicate the time until Christmas Day. Recently this custom came to a large city church and to its families with children of grade school age and younger.

On the first Sunday afternoon of December about a hundred parents, children, and teachers gathered in the social hall for a family Advent celebration. They found small tables set with materials for the making of a wreath by each family. The aroma of evergreen filled the air. Three large tables were loaded with a variety of fresh greens cut and brought from the country by several families. Various games were placed around the room: a Christmas crossword puzzle on a bulletin board, Christmas masterpieces in picture puzzles, a Pin-the-star-on-the-tree game, a wreath relay. The ministers joined fathers and children in the relay until they all saw that punch was being served. Small boys found it great fun to select homemade cookies from a Christmas cooky tree. But eating gave way to singing when the organist at the piano and a teacher with a guitar began playing carols. The song sheet included kindergarten songs as well as carols.

The liveliest time of all was when each family worked on its Advent wreath. Every wreath was different and every one was beautiful. Some were made of pine and laurel, some of spruce, others of fir and ground pine. Some had four red candles, others had white candles, one had symbolic pink and lavender.

During this entire time brothers and sisters three years of age and younger had a party and playtime in another room with their teachers.

But when the wreath-making was finished their mothers went for them and they joined their families for closing worship. It was led by a family of four, each of whom took part in the service, which had been mimeographed, made into booklets, and given to everyone. When the father lighted one candle on the wreath for the first Sunday of Advent every family lighted a candle on its own wreath. The reading of the Old Testament prophecy seemed to be fulfilled in the living tableau of the Holy Family that appeared when the curtains were pulled back. A hush fell over the candlelit room. All eyes watched Mary and Joseph by the manger. Everyone sang "Silent Night! Holy Night!" and the family Advent celebration ended.

This event was planned for the purpose of fellowship and worship by families within the larger church family. When one looks at it carefully these elements can be found:

> Persons used all their senses: tasting, touching, hearing, smelling, seeing.
> They expressed themselves freely in playing games, singing, speaking, reading, making something with their hands.
> They worshiped as family units.
> The worship booklet and wreath that were carried to each home motivated family worship during the month.

With so much involvement demanded of every person, or permitted for every person by nature of the program, it was not surprising that this event was long remembered and highly appreciated.

It was reported that a three-year-old whispered to her mother during the tableau, "Where are the ox and ass?" From her memory of stories, pictures, or songs it was evident that she was putting ideas together. A two-year-old looked up transfixed at the first tableau she had ever seen and exclaimed, "Mrs. Jesus." In the past few weeks she had learned to use the prefix Mrs. with her teachers' names. Now she used it as she related this living picture to her first storybook of the birth of Jesus.

A nine-year-old came alone. Her parents had made reservations but as was so often the case they could not quite manage it, so again she was a "loner." Another family included her at their table and assisted her in making her wreath. The teacher who played the guitar strolled among the tables as he sang "The Friendly Beasts" and encouraged others to sing. He stopped at one table and asked a girl to sing one verse alone with him. He did not know that her family was facing its first Christmas without their father, who had recently died. A grandmother, with no children living close by, made the punch and set the serving table assisted, by the nurse from the crib-toddler room. Another brought the cooky tree. When one had eyes to see, there were many subtle and tangible things happening to people that afternoon.

A few months later as some adults were remembering the family Advent celebration, one father said: "It set the tone for the whole Christmas season in our home. It pinpointed meanings that are apt to get bypassed in a commercial Christmas. The girls were anxious to use the worship booklet every Sunday." Others said: "The timing was good—the children did not get restless because they were doing something all the time"; "We liked it because there are so few places where you can take the whole family. Five-year-old Cathy has felt left out of church affairs because her brother who is nine goes to Junior Club every Saturday. Children are anxious to participate even at kindergarten age."

Here was a congregation living its faith with its children—helping them to be conscious of how church families celebrate Christmas, teaching them that Christmas is a time to remember God's gift of Jesus. Many churches celebrate Advent, but some feel that such family experiences need to be found for other times of the year as well. So they are experimenting with what can be meaningful for children and youth in relationship with adults during Lent, at Pentecost, and on Worldwide Communion Sunday.

Today's Child

The child and youth of today are growing up in an atmosphere of national and world progress, uncertainty, and strife. They are exposed to more knowledge than their parents were as children through television, movies, supermarkets, travel, shopping centers, world fairs, and expositions. Many have already lived in two or more cities. But with their expanded world they see and hear and feel tension on all sides, even in school and church. Their parents and teachers are under untold pressures because of changes in their adult lives. Their older brothers may be part of the student rebellion. But this is the era of child and youth: it is their time. They are not practicing or preparing for life; this is life itself.

Today's Adult

Adults have problems of their own to deal with, even while living with the young. The parents and grandparents of today's child are wrestling with new knowledge, new culture patterns, and a new style of living. Perhaps dreams of what it would be like to be a father or a mother are not coming true. Perhaps grandparents, in turn, are putting pressure on parents for the old style of life. Both need to be realistic and to face tensions, seeking causes and trying to deal with them practically. Only then are they free and open to learn from each other as well as from the young. Parents and teachers no longer need to be the final source of information, but rather, interpreters and guides to other sources. These roles, of interpreter and guide, make it possible for adults to live with the knowledge explosion. For after all, this is the era of adults also. This is their time; they too are living now. Indeed, some of them are responsible for creating technological change itself.

It may be said that maturity is an achievement of persons who are not bound by the past but have learned to receive and examine newness—to evaluate it in the light of the past, to reject and accept parts of it. Such persons live and teach with open, exploratory minds, whether parent or teacher. Their contribution to today's child and youth may be to foster within them the attitudes and abilities that make it easy for them also to receive and examine newness or change. A basic way of working toward that end is one of providing experiences through the senses wherein creativity, originality, and flexibility are expected and appreciated by adults. In an atmosphere of acceptance and trust, creative thinking and creative expression may be achieved by the young and help them to cope with the unknown future.

Learning Through the Senses

Leisurely sit and observe a baby. His world is new and strange, but he starts to investigate it immediately. He goes about learning of his surroundings through the use of all his senses. His every movement is sensory—looking at his hands, putting them in his mouth, reacting to a noise. Learning about his world and about himself is a long, slow process, but he does most of it by seeing, hearing, touching, tasting, and smelling in relationship to other persons. Each bit of experience adds to others to help him find meaning. For example, he has felt himself to be a part of his mother for a long time but he gradually discovers that he is a separate self with hands that he controls, with food that he alone eats, with eyes and ears that see and hear mother as separate and apart from him. He needs many, many experiences during his early years for this discovery of himself, for the building of self-esteem and self-confidence.

He also will find out through his senses what other persons and the world around him are like. Who are they? What will they do to me? Will I like them? How do we deal with one another? What is sand, sun, rain, wind? City and farm, land and sea, space? What a big, wide, wonderful world there is to discover! Who made it? All this he does through perceptual learning. Different sensory reactions combine, past experience is added, and gradually the young child begins to comprehend a person, an object, action, or idea; that is, he begins to form concepts.

Let us look briefly at the concept of the church and how a growing child could acquire his concept through perceptual learning. It might be something like this:

> He will hear the word "church" when taken there for child care as an infant.
> He will be fed.
> He may hear soft music.

He is handled gently but firmly.

He misses his mother.

He cries.

Some months later he will rebel and not want to go.

Still later he will ask, "Go church today?"

Church is a happy place.

He asks about it every day.

If he is fortunate, this place will be one where he moves about to play with a truck, ride a trike, look at a picture book, fix a puzzle, eat a cooky. He is free but he does not always get his own way. Adults help him. There are other children his size.

One spring day when riding on a bus he surprises his mother by waving his hand and exclaiming, "There's my church!"

But he is puzzled the next Sunday when she takes him there and says, "Daddy and I are going to church now." He may wonder, "Aren't we already at church?" His teacher helps him: "They are going to the room where the organ is playing and big folks are singing." It takes a long time to know that "church" can mean "morning worship." Sometimes his mother takes him there with her.

He becomes a block builder and he builds a church. He puts many rooms in it because he knows that babies, children, and grown-ups all are in the church.

He has a snack with other children in his room. He smells the apple slices before eating.

He draws a picture of his church.

He learns a song about the church.

Once his teacher took the children to the organ when the organist was there. He played their very own songs and they sang. Another day they went to the minister's study and talked with him.

On some occasions he goes to the church with his parents on a week-night to have dinner with church people. He knows many grown-ups at church. In fact, one day he found that the man who greeted him every Sunday at the church door was a clerk in the supermarket. He found an old friend in a new place.

Eventually he will come to know that the church is more than a building and more than a morning service of worship. It is people who believe certain things and act in special ways.

The concept of the church grows with many experiences, planned and unplanned. Perceptual learning may make the concept one of warmth and happiness or it may bring negative meanings: his concept will fluctuate. Part of his church concept will deal with God, Jesus, love, forgiveness as he begins to build meanings in these concepts also. It will take a long, long time for the child to know the church as the body of Christ.

"What he feels, tastes, smells, hears, and sees rapidly becomes a part of 'that child who goes forth every day,' and as he gives expression to it through sound, word, or color, it becomes his art. The foundation of scientific understanding and aesthetic appreciation and expression lies, then, in the small child's sensory experiences, which start long before nursery school."[1] The impact of early learning on the intellectual and emotional growth of a child is vital for his understanding of himself and the world in which he lives. While such learning may not be considered "religious learning" it really lays the foundation for making religion possible in coming years. The first years of life are every bit as important as the school years, if not more so, for conceptual learning.

Learning through the senses continues for a lifetime. In fact, sense experiences are absolutely essential for an adult's well-being and emotional satisfaction. Sometimes an inner restlessness can be gratified through beautiful music, fascinating art, gourmet foods, delightful scents, or opportunities to create something with one's hands.

Planning for Sensory Learning

Sensory learning is basic for persons of all ages. And the more senses used the better the learning. In the history of the Sunday church school, hearing is the sense that was used most frequently. The learners listened when the teacher spoke. Sometimes he reinforced his speaking with a picture so that the learners could use their eyes to catch meanings. But history has shown that extremely limited learning takes place under such teaching efforts.

Today there is emphasis on perceptual learning wherein a person uses his whole self in the process of building ideas or concepts. Both church and secular educators are working on a comparatively new philosophy of education dealing with the discovery of meaning. They are working on the use of "key concepts" for their religious resource materials and their general education curricula. They believe that the teaching of key concepts in each given body of knowledge will give persons a fundamental understanding of that subject, and a framework on which to build ever-deepening meanings. Before entering first grade a child has quite a hoard of information that he works with to build general ideas or concepts. As he grows and learns he gradually puts together what he discovers about a given object, tests his information as he goes along, sees parts within a whole, generalizes, and evaluates. This is what the young child, mentioned earlier, was doing as he discovered meanings for the word "church." He modified early ideas, he clarified later information, and his concept of the church will continue to change as further experiences and insights come to him.

Experiences are the stuff from which concepts grow, and experiences are man's reaching out to see and hear, to smell and taste, to touch the environment of persons and things in which he finds himself, and becomes involved. Early educators of the young child such as Froebel, Montessori, and Hill recognized that sensory experiences could and did contribute to intellectual development, so they were built into the curricula for kindergarten and early grades. In high schools and colleges teachers have primarily used experiences of hearing for their students, which meant that teachers lectured. But today, even in colleges, some teachers are making concerted efforts to stimulate as many senses as possible. Recently when students in a well-known university were studying the Civil War and debating its issues, they also heard music from that period and tasted corn bread made from a recipe of that time.

Conceptualizing is an individual process, so within any group of children, youth, or adults each person is at a different level or stage of generalizing particular ideas. Teachers must realize that they are teaching individuals, not a class, and make allowances for individual backgrounds. They plan a variety of sensory experiences and provide materials, space, and time for each person to do his own learning. Discovery of meanings may come through working with clay, through painting, or through role-playing. When a great variety of creative work is available persons choose according to mood. Often they join others in group projects, group research, and group discussion. Whichever it is, the involvement of each and every learner is essential: perceiving, reacting, thinking, expressing, and, hopefully, acting on meanings found. Teachers are challenged in this kind of teaching to provide suitable materials and resources, to hear and watch individual learners, and to guide group thinking and action.

Adults Who Plan

When the first rocket blasted into space, a ten-year-old boy said, "Maybe they'll pierce heaven and find God." And a woman com-

mented: "I think this space exploration is all wrong. Man is invading God's territory." Both comments indicate what each was thinking about God and his place in the universe. Probably neither comment would be made today, but both were products of a certain kind of teaching in regard to the concept of heaven.

In order to plan for others, adults need to analyze themselves, their religious beliefs, and their methods of teaching. Many parents and teachers have found that they have to unravel wrong ideas and discard misconceptions. In the words of a city-bred child, "The first thing to do when building a new house is to tear down the old one." The process of adjusting to newness goes on and on. Those who teach must be good adjusters—recognizing new knowledge and dealing with it to the best of their ability. This includes new information on how to communicate.

how to teach. Some will find it very difficult to discard favorite methods. Many adults are loathe to relinquish the power of the lecture method wherein they control the situation and have ample opportunity to speak. Others still teach as they were taught, which usually includes memorization by rote and art expression with patterns. And there are some who believe that they can teach in the church with little or minimum preparation, if only they are believing Christians.

But adults who teach must be in contact with all the exhilarating or the degenerating changes in the world. They must be aware and weigh values. They must experiment with teaching methods, be original, appreciate originality in others. When they take risks with new materials and practices they need the support and approval of the teaching staff. They need to be open to modern history, music, Biblical scholarship, science, drama, art, poetry, so they know what is going on and what is the "normal" world of the younger generation. They should open themselves to what is happening: they shall listen and truly hear, look and truly see, touch and really feel. There is much to be unlearned and much to learn. But adults who teach are in a position to enjoy both, over and above the inevitable growing pains, because they realize that they must be facilitators of growth for others.

This book is about such teachers and leaders in the church who try to work realistically with persons through experiences that provide perceptual learning. They have discovered that sensory and expressional experiences within a group add a new dimension to verbal learning and to verbal relationships between persons.

2
Seeing Is Remembering

A young child sat weekly with his parents in a church pew near a stained-glass window depicting the young shepherd David. He always watched it change color as the sun shone on it or clouds obscured the sun's rays. He began naming the different colors he saw, and asked his mother to tell him those he could not identify.

Seeing takes on deeper meaning when other persons share comments, add facts, or correct misunderstandings. One Sunday morning the boy's first-grade teacher took the class into the sanctuary to inspect this beautiful window. As the children looked at it, she told them the story of the friendship between David and Jonathan. Learning these new details added interest to the window. It made the boy think of his best friend. During the week he said to his mother, "I'm going to be a friend with Alfred like Jonathan and David."

Later, when he and his father read together the story of the Goliath incident, he began to admire David for the courage and skill he showed. In high school he came to see David as a special king and the one to whom God revealed his covenant with man. Still later, as he looked at the window, he saw the whole range of David's personality down to his deceit, lust, and plotting of murder. As the boy matured in years and knowledge, he saw ever-deeper meanings in what caught his eye.

Many churches have beautiful windows, architectural points of interest, and symbolic religious carvings that are rarely seen with more than a roving, impatient eye. Other churches that are plain in structure and furnishings also have objects worth seeing, such as, the pulpit Bible, the minister's Bible which is usually well worn and marked, the baptistry with its font or bowl, the book of baptism wherein names are written of persons when baptized, the Communion ware and its history, and the book that records the names of church members. It takes an alert teacher to help others see significant representations and records of the Christian faith.

To See or Not to See

Persons react to only a small portion of all that goes on around them. The place where they are and the direction in which they look determines what they may receive at a given moment. This fact motivates the team of junior teachers in a New York City church. Because of alert and ingenious teachers their whole room literally speaks as one enters. Books with pictures appropriate to a given session are opened and stood up on table and windowsill. Palestinian costumes are draped over a screen with pottery jugs set beside them. The children help make the bulletin board and change it often as their study progresses. When creative art work is planned the materials are put on tables and arouse curiosity when children arrive. Usually one screen illustrates the hymn that is being learned. Recently this hymn was "All Creatures of Our God and King." The lead teacher put the hymn title in large letters across a screen and tacked appropriate nature pictures underneath. In front of the screen she placed a table with interesting bits of God's creation: seashells, coral shells, antlers, fossils, and some tiny shells only one eighth of an inch in size. The magnifying glass added to the wonder and appreciation of these items. This display made the words of the hymn more meaningful and the appreciation of these city children more real as they sang wholeheartedly, "O praise him! O praise him! Alleluia!" Compare the perceptual learning that may take place in this room with that in a room that is never changed. In many churches children return each Sunday to the same map, the same picture, and a blank chalkboard.

Project Head Start of the Federal Government has made many observations in its short life and one of them is: "Disadvantaged children come with unseeing eyes, unhearing ears, and unsmelling noses." A Chicago church[2] situated among such children worked out its summer program in a thoughtful and sensitive manner. Rather than taking the youngsters to the country and the woods, they decided to help them have a positive experience of their immediate world, the city. Within this theme they would also deal with beauty, personal worth, justice and injustice, interpersonal relationships. The staff worked hard. They helped these children to see the beauty of sunset colors through the black design of a fire escape, to make mobiles with broken glass found in the street, to watch a person walk and try to determine how he feels by his walk, to visit the Urban League and see for themselves what goes on there. Finding the most in everyday surroundings helped unseeing eyes to see.

"A picture is worth ten thousand words" goes the timeworn Chinese proverb. This aptly describes an "unreadable" book entitled *Libro Illegible*.[3] Rather than a text composed of words this story is carried by different colored pages, holes in some pages, and a red thread. And it *can* be understood as one looks carefully to see honestly. Another illustration of the Chinese proverb might be a church teacher who speaks little but is understood by a glance, a wink, a frown or a smile, a pat on the shoulder, a stern or a sympathetic eye. Whether they like it or not, teachers are examples. So are parents and leaders of groups and committees. Part of a child's learning is the process by which the behavior of the adult affects his behavior and causes change. He *sees* what the adult does and it affects him more strongly than anything spoken. Apparently Louise had been so affected by her kindergarten teacher that, one Sunday when she was lost from her father and crying in the hallway, she stopped weeping on seeing her teacher. Hand in hand they went in search of Father. After finding him, Louise beamingly exclaimed: "Look, Daddy! See what I found." She no longer had any notion of having been lost. She was secure with her teacher.

Television has brought the entire world so close to families that even children under six talk about faraway places and people. Today many nursery schools and kindergartens have a world globe in their rooms. Children look and ask questions. "My daddy's in Hawaii. Where's that?" "I was in Spain last summer. Where's Spain?" With such and many more comments from her class, one teacher decided to use the globe to introduce her story at Christmastime. She began by saying: "I want to tell you about a man who used to live in a country across the ocean from America. He lived right here," and she pointed to Israel. She went on about what the man did before she mentioned his name. From a historic place and time she got to the fact of Christmas being a time to remember his birth date because of his importance as a man. "Seeing is believing"? At least the globe helped to make the story factual.

A teacher of three-year-olds recently went on an ocean trip and had to say good-by to her little friends. On the first Sunday she was absent the lead teacher showed the children a letter that Mrs. Burns had sent to them.

Dear 3's:

I have been busy this week packing for my trip

Can you tell Mrs. Winchester some of the things I am taking with me on the ship?

I have put in one picture of something I am not going to take along. Can you tell what one I am not going to take?

Your friend and teacher,
Mrs. Burns

She had clipped from magazines these pictures for the children to name: toothbrush, sweater, shoes, camera, swimsuit, pajamas, raincoat, wallet, and a big, fat rooster. These children saw with their eyes, named the objects, and enjoyed the joke their teacher had sent them.

Looking and Perceiving

Continual use of eyes sometimes makes sight very superficial: one looks but does not see. In a ten-day junior camp the leaders used "eyes" as a focal point to help city children look at the woods and lake with discernment. Name tags pictured a human eye followed by the word "am," after which each child wrote his own name and colored the eye to match his own. Their first games used the eyes in particular and the director's first words of greeting were centered on eyes. He gave some details of their physiological construction and the children were amazed at the functions their eyes perform. They were interested too in how a camera is made to reflect pictures much as the eye does its work. On succeeding days the children were asked to look for particular things such as: what they saw on the nature trail, persons they saw in the dining room, ways to help another camper, ways someone helped them. As the camp progressed, the children became more sensitive to what was happening around them and what meaning it had for them.

A person can look and not perceive, or he can hear and touch without perceiving. To perceive is to obtain knowledge. When a person looks at someone or something and perceives, he is aware of their existence and some of their characteristics. He has some kind of understanding of them because he looks with inquiry; he does not look passively. For example, a family on their first auto trip across the United States may look passively at scenery similar to their own area but will notice differences and ask questions about radically different geographic formations. In a class of eleven-year-olds who were studying the events of Holy Week one boy looked at a picture of Jesus praying, "Not my will but thine be done," and asked, "Why did Jesus have to die?" Both instances are examples of the process of perceiving, of perceptual learning.

Television brings pictures into homes, schools, and churches every day. There is no doubt about the fact that learning takes place from watching television. The big question is that of determining what should be shown for positive effect and what omitted because it is harmful. The history of the civil rights movement as shown on television during the past six years has awakened the public to existent conditions. What the cameras caught in a succession of pictorial events made a far greater impact than radio or the printed page. People have been aroused by the injustices and brutalities of man to man. A group of concerned youth saw such a program and it motivated them into action in their own locality. The inequities they found had been so glossed over by officials that they discovered a long-term project for themselves on behalf of others.

New churches are going up everywhere, but only a few congregations have used the experience for memorable learning. Recently a crowd of grown-ups and children was seen on the site of a half-finished church. The workmen managing the huge cranes kept working and did not seem to mind the crowd. On second sight, it was noticeable that this was an organized crowd—boundaries had evidently been set and no one exceeded them. But there was high enthusiasm. Finally a shout was heard, "There it goes!" then, utter silence. The crane moved slowly but surely as it carried the slim, modern steeple upward. Old and young alike watched; they cheered as it was fastened into place by the workmen on the roof. But they did not leave—there was more to watch! And in another half hour the crane lifted a workman in a hanging seat. In front of him was a copper cross which was held by wires from the crane. This was most precarious work—to bolt the steel base of the cross into the tip of the steeple. The families were intent on the work and when it was completed someone spontaneously started singing the Doxology. It was the sight of a lifetime! Here and now, in this community, these children, youth, and adults had placed the symbol of their faith for all to see. The day had been discussed and anticipated for a long time and it would certainly be remembered.

In a New England church a young pastor has instituted a Maundy Thursday tenebrae service. The word "tenebrae" refers to the special songs and prayers for the last three days of Holy Week and comes from the third or fourth century. Following the Lord's Supper, the laymen who served it are seated at a table placed lengthwise at the head of the center aisle. The minister lights eight tall candles on the table and places another candle on the Communion table. Each man reads a passage of Scripture relative to Jesus' last week. After each passage the reader pauses and snuffs out a candle. Simultaneously some of the electric lights are turned off. Finally, the only light in the sanctuary is the one candle on the Communion table behind which the minister stands. Without a word, he snuffs out that light and the people are in darkness for a minute or more, then he relights it. What eyes perceived was an impressive symbol of the dark agony of the crucifixion and the return of hope in the light of the resurrection.

On occasion a certain minister asks the congregation to close their eyes during the reading of the Scripture or the singing of an anthem. They have discovered that they not only hear better but make mental images and when they open their eyes again they perceive more keenly.

Graphic Art

Graphic art is an acknowledged aid to teaching. A church school teacher in Chicago who took her class to the Art Institute was surprised to learn from its educational director that of all the hundreds of groups visiting the Institute hers was the first Protestant church group. It is hoped that during the ten years since then more Protestant leaders have taken their classes on guided tours of the Institute.

In the United States and Canada alone there are over three hundred art museums. Add to this the number of exhibits in colleges and universities, as well as numerous private galleries, and one can see that fine art is available to a large proportion of the population of these two countries without having to go to European and other art centers.

Sometimes schools and churches have their own exhibits. In one church where senior highs have been given time and materials to paint Biblical meanings, they exhibit the pictures occasionally. Families enjoy them and even the youngest children take a walk with their teachers to see the pictures. When a special collection of Christmas pictures by artists around the world was exhibited, classes visited it, too, and looked carefully, in order to learn and to appreciate.

Most Westerners are accustomed to seeing Jesus and the Holy Family portrayed as white people, often in Italian Renaissance setting. It is important that children and youth be exposed to the Biblical paintings of Asians and Africans so they can appreciate the universality of the Christ as he becomes one with the artist in any given culture. People near Birmingham, Alabama, may want to visit the 16th Street Baptist Church to see a work of art. A stained-glass window shows an agonized Negro Jesus being pounded by water from fire hoses. It is done in blues and purples. The people of Wales gave it to the church when it had to rebuild after a bomb explosion that killed four girls. The gift was possible through ten thousand small contributions of Welsh people who cared for Christians overseas.

One of the teacher's tasks is to help students visualize the lands of the Bible through graphic means: pictures, objects, maps, time lines, and modes of dress. Junior and junior high classes especially like to piece together a time line of Biblical events and personalities. A time line marked off on a long, horizontal strip of paper by centuries, with historical events and personages indicated on it, illustrates at a glance that Abraham lived about as many years before the time of Jesus as we are living after.

A teacher of an adult Bible study group found such a time line useful in her class. She stretched a strip of adding machine paper across the wall, writing in at the ends the years 2,000 B.C. and 4 B.C., respectively. Class members scanned their study material for names and corresponding dates to insert chronologically. The idea sparked their interest and imagination, and they kept a time line during the whole six months of their course. The plain strip of adding machine paper became a treasury of historical events. One member remarked, "I've never seen Old Testament history so clearly."

A teacher who has visited the Holy Land uses her Kodachrome slides in short sequences for various groups as needed. At Christmas she shows the road from Jerusalem to Bethlehem with the shepherds' field in a broad valley and explains that this route might have been taken by the Wise Men. Her pictures of Jericho and the dig there not only enhance Old Testament learning but show the country described in Jesus' story of the good Samaritan. The town where Mary, Martha, and Lazarus lived seems more authentic and the walk from Jerusalem more realistic with her pictures of the area and the road over the hill from the Mount of Olives.

Modern drawings of Biblical events are sensitively done in two filmstrips[4] suitable for use with adults and youth at Advent and Pentecost. Both show the people involved in these events as the rugged peasants they were. The accompanying script on a record interprets the true meaning in each event and adds proper musical accompaniment.

Many teachers use maps to indicate where the church at large, and their church in particular, is at work. Persons living in the western hemisphere are accustomed to seeing their part of the world on the left of the map and the eastern half on the right. They are usually surprised to know that Asians see the map in reverse, with the East shown on the left and the West on the right. It is good to see the world from an Asian perspective.

Trips Are for Seeing

Trips are an excellent means of seeing for oneself. On a visit by one junior department to a Jewish synagogue, the children were impressed by the rabbi's opening the doors of the ark and removing the Torah from its beautiful covering. They listened attentively as he read from it the same words they had read in the book of Deuteronomy. They asked about the six-pointed star in one of the stained-glass windows, and heard about the meaning of the Star of David.

Another class visited the synagogue during the Festival of Booths (Sukkoth), which is the traditional Hebrew thanksgiving celebration. The booth, or sukkah, was made of evergreens hung with fruits and vegetables. The children had been prepared for what they saw by their teacher, who explained this ancient custom and read some of the Sukkoth prayers.

For many people in isolated villages or rural areas it is impossible to plan such trips because of distances. But other kinds may be feasible such as visits to the home of a Jewish or Catholic family to learn about their faiths. Here one might see a mezuzah and prayer shawl, a rosary and crucifix. There might even be an art object such as a passover plate or icon, family heirlooms from the old country.

Trips to points of special interest are instructive for teachers and young people alike. A unique part of one New England church is the old millstone embedded in the floor in front of the Communion table. Meant to symbolize bread, it also is a reminder of the church's founding days.

Trips to visit the mission work of the church are often possible to arrange. Young people studying some of the social problems faced by the church are eager to glimpse firsthand the work being done in depressed areas both in the large cities with mixed ethnic populations and in the isolated rural areas. This interest makes it possible for church leaders to arrange chartered bus tours to mission centers during the summer vacation. When a person actually sees how the church is meeting human needs then he is more eager to help.

Where it is not possible to take a trip, the second-best way for students to see the "real thing" is to have visitors come to the class. In many churches some member of the congregation who has been in other countries, either as a tourist or on business, can bring objects of historical interest or show colored slides.

One man, traveling in the Holy Land, picked up a stone in the creek bed where David is supposed to have found his for the battle with Goliath. It was smooth and round, of four-inch diameter. He brought it to his church school class, and, of course, let the children hold it. He was secretly amused to watch as each of the boys "wound up" as if to throw it, believing himself for that one minute to be the hero David. Perhaps holding and feeling the stone meant as much to the boys as seeing it. Feeling is important to all of us, but especially to the blind.

Seeing Without Eyesight

A person with normal sight is amazed at the abilities of a person without sight. Although a blind person uses the words, "Let me see it," his actual perception is through the other four senses. His "seeing" comes primarily through touching as he learns to use braille, and to feel objects that help him to "see."

Relief maps are of value to everyone but particularly to blind persons. These are the maps they can "see" as they trace their fingers gently over mountains and lakes. A church school teacher who had a blind girl in his class was aware of her need to "see" with her hands and helped his pupils to understand. The class made a relief map of Palestine and included her in the project as they made the contours and rivers. When the juniors visited the church sanctuary to study a stained-glass window, they took her close enough to feel the leaded panes.

To make class experiences as normal and meaningful as possible the teacher kept in close contact with her parents. From them he learned when she first inquired about the cross and how the parents had taken her to the church to "see" it and explained the historical meaning of the cross. When she asked about the service of the Lord's Supper, she was permitted to hold the cup and bread after the service, and with the minister she examined the Communion table, the cloth covering, the plates, and the chalice. Her parents explained their symbolic meaning. Members of the congregation gradually became aware of how they too could relate to this child and help her "see."

When eight-year-old Tommy was graduated from the primary department his church presented him with braille copies[5] of Matthew and Mark instead of the usual Bible given to the other children. His parents and school teacher were consulted as to which type of braille he could read so the proper edition would be purchased. A year later his class secured for him a braille hymnal.[6] Tommy did much of the classwork but always had special enthusiasm for making things with his hands out of clay, felt, styrofoam, and papier-mâché.

In different cities there are interesting places for blind persons to visit such as: libraries with books and magazines recorded on tapes or records as well as in braille, an art museum,[7] with objects accessible for touching and identified with braille labels, a garden with terraced beds at waist height so the scent and the feeling are within reach. A college girl once "adopted" two blind children for Saturdays and took them many places. What they enjoyed most was a visit to a farm where they held baby chicks, patted cows, and examined fences of wood and stone. Anyone who knows a blind person realizes how much he learns from him, and what an asset he would be in a church group, like the blind woman who had the whole dinner table laughing at church one night. Checkerboard ice cream was served and she said, "Now as for me I'd like plaid ice cream—a good Scotch plaid."

Leaders Too Must See

Church leaders and teachers often seek experiences of seeing for their own knowledge and inspiration. To see the ugliest section of one's hometown as well as the most beautiful makes a person sensitive to the needs of humans for decent living. To visit a studio where stained-glass windows are made helps one appreciate the fine art of working with glass. To see an original painting brings depth of feeling not known in looking at a reproduction. There are two special originals that are on exhibit only six weeks each year. These are the Munkácsy paintings of *Christ Before Pilate* and *Descent from the Cross,* which are exhibited publicly during Lent each year in the John Wanamaker store of Philadelphia, Pennsylvania. The experience of seeing these life-size canvases is one of deep perceptual learning.

In this day of television, movies, travel, and cultural interchange the church must use every opportunity to help young and old look more closely at the world around them to see human similarities and needs, to remember, to act.

3

To Hear or Not to Hear

The teacher stopped talking. The noise from the junior department in the next room seemed unusually loud. In the brief interval during which she waited to make herself heard, six-year-old Isabel turned to her wide-eyed and said, "Isn't that bee-oo-oo-tiful?"

The teacher's annoyance was the child's pleasure, for she was listening to hymn-singing such as she had never before heard. The teacher was jolted awake to a new angle of teaching and she said in response: "Yes, Isabel, that music is beautiful. Let's all listen to it for a while."

In that one instant the teacher came to understand that her voice was not the only important sound to be heard by her class. By listening to the hymn-singing of the juniors, her group was gaining a wider concept of the church. She let them listen to the juniors on other Sundays, and once the primaries visited the juniors during worship time so that they might praise God with older boys and girls. Listening became, much more broadly than before, a method of learning. The teacher did not ask the children to listen only to her, but arranged for them to listen to many people and many things.

Hearing is a selective process; a person chooses what he wants from all the sounds about him. When Isabel chose to hear the music she "tuned out" the voice of the teacher. This is an interesting characteristic of hearing; one cannot tell what another person is listening to by looking at him. A minister claims that many in his congregation turn off their hearing during the sermon and others turn off during the music. They look attentive but their minds are elsewhere.

A World Alive with Sounds

Interesting research in hearing is currently taking place in New York

City. A doctor records the sound of a mother's heartbeat, then has it piped into the hospital nursery bed of her newborn infant. The rhythmical sound is one to which the baby has been accustomed for nine months. The doctor believes it may comfort the child and help him adjust in a new, strange world.

Hearing is one of the most useful ways in which we learn about our environment. We hear radio, television, and record players. We hear the roar of automobile throughways and powerful jets. On occasion, if we listen, we may hear the silence of the forest or the chatter of goldfinch and chipmunk. We hear lectures, concerts, and operas.

Some of this hearing is inattentive, and justifiably so. To keep sane or calm a person is forced to tune out sounds such as the neighbor's barking dog, street traffic, air traffic, machinery at one's job, the television at home when another member of the family wants a program. When a student needs to concentrate he does not hear much of what goes on around him. The ability to "tune out" or "turn off" one's hearing is a protection for a person.

But some inattentive hearing may cause trouble. Have you not had the experience of talking with a person who only half hears what you say? This causes a strain in the relationship between you. Or have you been caught in not hearing what a child was trying to tell you? A father tells that his only traffic offense was due to his not listening as he parked the car. His five-year-old in the back seat asked, "What does that sign say?" The sign was about parking regulations, but the father had not heard the child speak.

Learning to Listen

There are times when it is important to give attention, listen intently, and register that which we hear. Some sounds are signals that require certain action. A church school superintendent remembers well the distinctive fire gong and school bell in his boyhood community in Maine; but best of all was the sound of the church bell. When it first rang on a Sunday morning, it meant that the family must get ready for church. When it rang a second time, the children watched out the window for Grandmother to come in the buggy drawn by dappled Nell. By the time the bell rang again, they had traveled the three miles to their white-spired church.

The story is told that the spiritual "Steal Away to Jesus!" was the "church bell" for people working the Southern cotton fields. On the night they planned to gather for worship the leader would sing this song as he worked. Others who heard joined in the singing and the song moved onward through the huge fields. It became for them their signal or church bell for worship.

Learning to listen when others are speaking is an important part of one's education. In the business world an adult is often promoted in his job because he is able to listen and to react in accordance with what he hears. Children need to be taught to listen and perceive, to gain knowledge or appreciation from hearing. This kind of hearing can lead to action: a change of thought, a change of will, or even a change of deed. It is this kind of hearing which teachers hope for in their pupils. What is heard by a pupil in the classroom is of utmost importance, but he learns only from that to which he listens attentively.

Teachers know that one of their continuing problems is that of helping pupils listen to what is going on in class. A leader of a junior high class noticed that one boy had not paid attention to the Scripture-reading. He turned to the boy with sympathy, saying: "Tom, this passage from Romans wasn't very interesting to you, was it? Paul's words don't sound very important. I understand how you feel; they do seem strange. But listen to this! Here is the same passage written in words such as we use every day." Then he read from Rom., ch. 12, in the J. B. Phillips translation of the New Testament.

In this incident the teacher was trying to win back the listening attention of the pupil by identifying with his mood. Rather than saying, "Tom, will you listen now?" he admitted that the boy probably had good reasons for daydreaming. It worked! When the words were put in contemporary usage and the class thought of modern illustrations for the Biblical words, Tom heard and really listened.

A teacher of a senior high group noticed that his young people had been getting into heated debates, some hanging on to their warped viewpoints without listening to other opinions. He recalled something he had learned in his business conferences—a method called "feedback." In group discussion a person who wants to talk must first state what he heard the preceding person say. If his version is accepted, he may then make his own contribution. The teacher introduced this type of feedback in his church school class. The young people found that they seldom heard one another correctly. They had to listen with all their powers of concentration, both to the one who spoke first and to the one who followed and interpreted what he had heard. Even when one was not speaking, he could check his own interpretation against the one given. The young people gave analogies and examples of what they were trying to say in order to clarify their ideas. They enjoyed the challenge of good listening and found that this type of feedback helped them to hear accurately and to participate in profitable discussion.

Adults in many congregations today have opportunity to discuss the sermon immediately after service. This experience has shown some that they need to listen more carefully for the minister's real meanings if they are to ask questions of him later.

Even the Youngest Learn to Listen

The old saying "Little pitchers have big ears" reminds us of times when young children have heard parents or teachers say things that were not meant for them. But all young children do not hear that well. Timmy was only three in a church nursery school when the teacher discovered that he did not listen to her. It was evident, when she called in his home, that his parents had frustrated him with so many "noes" and "don'ts" that life seemed to hinder him on every side. So in order to do the things he felt compelled to do—feel, taste, try out, examine—he simply turned off his hearing and went about his own experimental business. "He's impossible!" exclaimed his mother. Parents and teacher together analyzed themselves and observed Timmy. They knew that they had to help him regain the ability to hear adults, so they spoke to him affirmatively and seldom, getting his undivided attention first.

In the informal nursery and kindergarten departments of church school, children begin the session in work centers of their choice. Of necessity there is a hum of conversation and laughter much of the time. If the teacher needs the attention of the whole group, she has methods by which to get it. In many children's rooms it is a common practice to have chords sounded on the piano as a signal to announce a change of activity. At the first chord the four-year-olds know it is almost time to jut away their work materials. When they hear it a second time, they begin to clean up their work centers.

One teacher planned a special experience for helping her children learn to listen. David wanted to bring his pet kitten to class, so she permitted him to do so. As the excitement and noise mounted, the cat looked for a place to hide. Later, when the children were eating cookies, David was able to get the cat from behind the block shelves. The teacher had prepared a saucer of milk. As she held the cat she suggested that everyone be quiet and listen to him lick up the milk. "It's a happy sound!" remarked one child. Then the cat settled down in the teacher's lap and purred. One by one the children tiptoed close to listen.

How much more effective is such a method of teaching children to listen than saying, "Keep still" or "Be quiet" or "Shut up." It becomes a challenge to listen for soft, barely audible sounds. Sometimes a class listens to the radiator sizzling, the clock ticking, the wind outdoors, the crunch of cookies at snack time. Or the teacher may make a game of listening, What am I doing now? From behind a screen or bookcase she will: crumple paper, tear paper, bounce a ball, ring a bell, bang two spoons or hit two blocks. These and other items may be put in a Sound Box and a child may choose something from the box to make a sound for others to guess. Sometimes the group will take a Listening Walk down the halls of a large church or outdoors, weather permitting.

A good story well told elicits keen listening every time. In a kindergarten group one Sunday every child was listening intently to the story. The teacher knew it well, and told it with sensitive concern for the man Bartimaeus. She varied the tone of her voice and the pace of her speaking. One could see that she enjoyed telling the story and reading part of it from Mark, ch. 1, in the direct and simple words of Today's English Version.[8] When she finished there was a satisfied sound of deep breathing. Then Christopher asked, "How could Jesus do that?" The teacher was secretly grateful for evidence that this boy was listening to perceive. So she answered him the best way she knew: "Jesus could heal Bartimaeus because God gave him the power to do it. Jesus was a special person. He was sent to show God's love and care for persons."

Musical Sounds Enrich Teaching

In a mission Sunday school in Nevada the teacher of juniors planned many experiences for pleasurable listening. When the children were studying about David and the Psalms, she brought a handmade flute similar to the kind used by Palestinian shepherds. The children in this foothill country knew about large sheep herds, but their study was enhanced by the music of the teacher's flute. It added a new dimension to their learning.

When the group studied Ps. 24 the teacher used choral speech. The ten juniors listened to the pitch of each other's voices as they decided with the teacher where each should sit so their voices would blend in tone. When it came time to try solo parts she let each child have a turn so that each could hear his own voice alone. Sometimes one child would become the audience—for the joy of listening to the verse choir.

Being part of a group singing hymns is not always uplifting. The teen-agers in a rural church were few in number and did not have a piano to use in church school. Their singing was self-conscious and labored. This changed when their teacher discovered that one of them played the guitar exceptionally well. She asked that boy to practice the Gloria and the Doxology. When guitar accompaniment was first used, the teacher asked the group to listen to it before singing. What about tempo; was it too slow? They sang together and decided on the best timing. The teacher spoke of the history of the Gloria, of the thousands of Christians who have worshiped God with its use down through the centuries. The young people sang with new enthusiasm as they heard fuller, richer music coming from their small group. When they tried the Doxology the teacher talked about that tune "Old Hundredth" and of the dignified but almost somber settings for Scripture in early hymns.

Today "Old Hundredth" has been made festive by Ralph Vaughan Williams, with horns and bass added to the basic theme. It was with keen excitement that a girl in the group reported some months later on a

television program showing a Catholic mission in Ghana. She was amazed and delighted with the rhythms and dance of these people as they sang, "All ye drummers praise the Lord."

Record Players and Tape Recorders

Record players and tape recorders may be used to great advantage in "listening times" both for music and for speaking. Many classes use tapes to record their own discussions or singing so that they can evaluate themselves later. Teachers who cannot sing use either or both to teach songs to children, to accompany their singing, and to provide music for creative rhythms. Several denominations publish records such as *Let's Sing Songs for Early Childhood* and *Let's Sing Songs and Hymns for Primary Children*[9] and *Kindergarten Songs, Games, and Rhythms*.[10]

Leaders of youth and adults have found records on church history pertinent in their teaching, such as *Great Decisions from Church History*[11] and *The Story Behind the Creeds* and *Sing Unto the Lord*[12]. Other series of curriculum materials include special recordings to fit the subjects being studied.

Another recording of interest is *Favorites of Gelineau Psalmody*,[13] in which the French Jesuit, Gelineau, has set psalms to music that congregations find singable. *Joy Is Like the Rain*,[14] an album of original songs in the folk style of our day, includes such numbers as: "It's a Long Road to Freedom," "Ten Lepers," "Spirit of God," and "Speak to Me, Wind." They are beautiful, timely, unforgettable, and useful in teaching situations.

There are times in a church when soothing music is needed to calm infants and toddlers. An unusual album *Golden Slumbers*[15] is a selection of lullabies from near and far with a description of each and a picture from that country.

The Use of Silence

In the *Arctic Odyssey,* a 1969 television documentary, the narrator reported the intensity of the cold and its demand for such heavy clothing that the men could barely hear one another speak. "Even the breathing of the dogs and the rumble of the sleds was softened by our parkas. I found that quiet was more overwhelming than the darkness or the cold." Men who have explored caves and canyons have also discovered that silence is difficult when one is conditioned to a world of lively sounds.

But many of them have come to appreciate it for the peace it gives them to think of the meaning of life and their relationship to God.

It is this peace which is held precious by Quakers who worship in silence except for brief speaking. Douglas Steere describes his experience in a leaflet entitled *A Quaker Meeting for Worship*. He explains: "I close my eyes, still my body, still my mind, and thank God for the week's happenings and what I've learned at his hand." He pauses to enjoy God, to search the past week, to hold up persons and situations. Distractions such as latecomers, two little girls, noisy cars, and wind seem to stir him to resolves and appreciations. "I resign myself to complete listening—letting go in the intimacy of this friendly company and in the intimacy of the Great Friend who is always near."

Some persons live with silence their whole lifetime because they are born with imperfect auditory nerves. Their eyes become as ears to them,

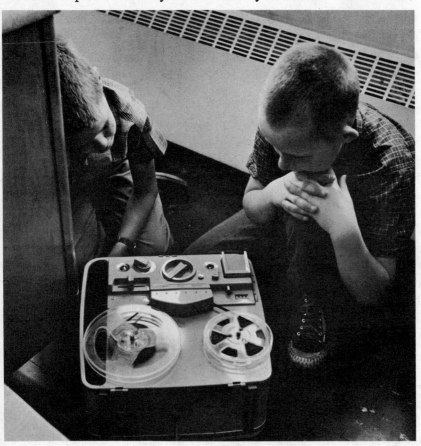

and when trained, they read lips to understand people as clearly as ears might hear them. A city church near a school for deaf children has for years provided chapel services for the boys and girls. The minister has used the stained-glass windows, Kodachrome slides, and filmstrips to help him give his message. Through the foresight of Charles Stanford, Jr., curator of education at the North Carolina Museum of Art, volunteers have learned to use sign language so that they can take the deaf on guided tours of the museum in Raleigh. (See note 7.) Church volunteers might do something similar in regard to Christian education and worship.

Perceptual learning through hearing is deeply appreciated when one thinks of living in silence. But Christian teachers might well cultivate in their groups the ability to learn through silence as well.

Teachers Learn to Listen

Upon her retirement a well-loved social worker was asked to tell her secret of success, that is, how she had been able to endear herself to so many hundreds of people. She had no sense of great accomplishment. She simply replied: "Each and every person I met said to me, 'Listen to my story.' And I listened."

If a teacher would help others listen, he himself should be able truly to hear. Some teachers suddenly become aware that they talk too much when they record a teaching session on a tape. Telling is not necessarily teaching. Listening with pupils may be a time when awe and wonder are savored, when deeper thinking can take place, when reverence is felt.

An impulsive talker is not really interested in other persons, for he must be the soloist and he alone knows the answers. Such a person will find it difficult to be a teacher, for a good teacher listens. He listens not only during class time but in the informality of the arrival and departure times. Students often come early to the church with news to tell, but will share it only when the teacher gives an attentive ear and concerned response. By his very manner such a teacher unconsciously teaches his class to become good hearers, to value one another, and to listen to individual thoughts and opinions. By providing a variety of hearing experiences, a teacher consciously teaches his pupils to become good listeners. He plans such experiences for himself as well, such as hearing symphonies and choirs, outstanding speakers and dramas. One teacher sought the sound of a waterfall in the heart of New York City. It was a brisk winter day and she had too much on her mind so she walked to Paley Park, a mini-park on a narrow lot where a building had been razed. She left the noisy traffic and sat down. Here she heard the music of a gentle, steady waterfall. Over a twenty-foot wall a curtain of water fell to the ledge and pool beneath. Its hush and lilt was indeed a curtain of sound, blocking out the surrounding city. For the moment the world within was at peace. After some time she went away with quickened step and mind.

An unusual experience of hearing and worshiping occurred to a missionary who spent two years in Chinese Communist prisons after the last war. He was facing his second Christmas in solitary confinement and wondered how he could celebrate the birth of the Christ. That night was Christmas Eve. On the still, dank air came Christmas carols sung in Chinese from a nearby cell. He joined in the singing and felt a keen, warm fellowship in this Advent worship with an unkown friend. The guards were unaware of the significance of songs interchanged. A week later when he was told to pack and be ready to leave, he wondered how he could say good-by to his newly found comrade. With a flash of inspiration, he whistled, "God be with you till we meet again." It was heard and understood. Back to him came the next words in Chinese, "By His counsels guide, uphold you." He faced an uncertain future strengthened by an experience of hearing.

4
Please Touch

What a delight it was to see a sign, PLEASE TOUCH. The exhibit room at the Museum of Contemporary Crafts in New York City was of irregular shape with subdued lighting and soft-colored spotlights. Openings of varied size and shape were cut in the temporary black walls. At every aperture a card identified the object and artist, with a duplicate card in braille, plus that special sign, PLEASE TOUCH. It made one feel almost giddy with anticipation. A framed picture painted with enamels on steel was smooth and cool as it lay horizontally in place. A child's chair of red fiber glass felt slippery and cold. A sculpture made of pony pelt and fox fur gave a warm, fuzzy sensation. In the center of the room stood a metal sculpture of a sea lion three feet tall. An adult put a hand in its mouth and invited a child nearby to try the same. He resisted until his mother was close at hand, then he too ventured and grinned. Every person there seemed utterly happy and free in being himself and enjoying art.

In most places we are confronted with signs, PLEASE DO NOT TOUCH. This is contrary to our natural instinct to reach out and feel with our fingers. An artist once confided that she is guilty of having touched some sculpture surreptitiously; at the time she felt impelled to learn and appreciate through her hands. She reports that she has often seen other people do it, too, when guards were elsewhere.

Understanding this human characteristic and working with it, instead of against it, has motivated many museums to put up signs by stuffed animals, FEEL OF ME or PAT ME. The Children's Museum in Jamaica Plain (Boston) was planned and built on the theory of learning through the senses. It has no collections under glass, no guards, no signs to be quiet or to keep hands off. It tries to make the world understandable to a child through perceptual learning. A child can see birds and insects in their natural forest habitat and then walk underground to see chipmunks and woodchucks in their burrows. He can put on the national garment of peoples of other countries. He can use a stone tool made by the Algonquin Indians. In a detailed exhibit called "What's Inside?" the curious child can at long last see and feel what is under a city street—sewer pipes, utility lines, manholes—as he walks down under.

Touching Things and Persons

Perceiving through the sense of touch is inborn, of course, as with all the senses. By the time most babies are four weeks old they will grasp anything their fingers touch. Increasingly thereafter they reach out with two hands to feel and examine things. When those hands are older they will do the same, as they feel of a fabric, of food, or of a tool when trying to decide on a purchase. Through touch we distinguish texture, weight, density, and form. Tactile learning begins in the crib and continues in spite of one's culture making it forbidden in some places.

As well as the discovery of things and how they work the tactual sense reacts to the human touch. A child wants to take the hand of parent or teacher. Something goes out of one's hand in touch: tangibility seems to be love. A teacher encourages a slow learner with a pat on the arm. Another helps a troubled teen-ager to stand taller with a tap on the back to commend his thinking. And still another warms the shocked heart of the widow by holding her firmly around the shoulders. The human touch can give reassurance, respect, and comfort without spoken words.

A visiting supervisor was expected at a church school one Sunday. When he entered the room of three-year-olds a little girl was crying lustily. The wise teacher quickly assessed the situation and said to the child, "Here comes a grandfather!" The girl looked, walked over to him, and held up her outstretched arms. The man said later: "I had never before seen the child. When I lifted her up she put her arms around my neck and settled into my shoulder. She seemed to want some security, and she found it." He patted her, walked to a mobile which they could push gently, talked with her softly, and in due time set her down. She was ready to "go it" alone.

Some Asian churches have a unique form of the benediction. At the close of worship when the peace is given, all take part. The giver places his right hand against the right palm of the receiver, and each closes the left hand over the other's right hand. The giver says in a low voice, "The peace of God be with you." The receiver then turns to the person next to him and gives the peace to him. In a large congregation the leader gives it to the first person in each pew who will then pass it on to the next person. In this tactual experience persons can feel truly "members one of another" as they speak God's blessing.

Biblical Perception Through Touch

Understanding the Bible more clearly sometimes comes through unexpected experiences. Mrs. Rowe will never forget the Sunday that Jay appeared in the primary department with radiant eyes, clutching an envelope in his hand. He glanced quickly around; he wanted everybody to see his prize. "See what I've got!" and he laid a small silver object dramatically on the table, then stood back in admiration.

"What's so special about that?" asked Joey. "Yeah, what is it anyway?" "It's got a star on it," added Tom, fingering the object.

"Where did you find it?" asked the teacher. "On the door of our new house," replied Jay. "It's the same thing we read about in that book last Sunday. You know—that thing people in Palestine have on their doors. They touch it every time they go into their houses. It has words printed on the inside, but I can't read them."

Jay's family had moved that week, and on moving day it was Jay who had spotted the mezuzah on the side of the door. He had learned about such at church school during the past month when his class had dramatized Palestinian family life. He slid open the silver case of the mezuzah and unrolled the piece of paper inside to show the printing.

"No wonder you couldn't read this, Jay. It is printed in the Hebrew language," said Mrs. Rowe. "But undoubtedly it says, 'Hear, O Israel: The LORD our God is one LORD; and you shall love the LORD your God with all your heart, and with all your soul, and with all your might.'

"But there is more than that. Let's look in our book of Deuteronomy and find out the rest of it." Mrs. Rowe picked up her Bible and read from Deut. 6:4–9 to find the directions for placing these words on a doorpost. Every child wanted to open and shut the mezuzah and feel of the scroll with the Hebrew words. The teacher was as excited as the children over Jay's prize, and she noticed that during the next few Sundays the experience with the mezuzah served as the real motivation for the children to memorize the Shema.

In another primary department the teacher asked if any children had access to objects from the Holy Land. One child brought an old Roman coin to church school. His father came, too, because the coin was said to be one that was in circulation at the time Jesus lived and hence very valuable. Each child held it carefully in his hands and looked closely at it. A teacher confided later, "Holding that coin, one that Jesus might possibly have held, somehow collapsed the centuries for me. For a few moments I was transfixed, and almost heard Jesus say: 'Render therefore to Caesar the things that are Caesar's, and to God the things that are God's.'"

Junior boys and girls came closer to Jesus' parable of the five wise maidens and the five foolish ones through inspection of an oil lamp discovered in an archaeological excavation in Palestine, and probably made as long ago as Jesus lived. They held it in their hands to feel its rough surface, and some of the children thrust their fingers into the hole in the top as the teacher explained how lighted wicks, drawing oil from such lamps, provided light for people's homes in ancient times. And it made them wonder what Jesus did as a boy in a house lighted so dimly after dark.

At Stamford, Connecticut, the chapel of a fairly new church building has an unusual wall with more than one hundred stones set in it. Located in the corridor separating the chapel from the library-lounge area, this wall has become a focal point of interest in the building complex. The stones trace the history of Christendom. They come from Bethlehem and Nazareth, from points on Paul's missionary routes, from Luther's church and home, from Canterbury, Notre Dame, Coventry, and other historic places. One stone bears the inscription: "These stones are from far places where other believers turned not their backs."

The stones were gathered by a former pastor who served with the U.S. Armed Forces overseas during World War II. He hoped that when his little church someday outgrew its building these stones would help twentieth-century Christians relate to the past. When the new building was erected the stones were set in the chapel wall.

Boys and girls have walked up to the stones and run their fingers over them. Adults have acknowledged that they, too, pause and ponder as they look at and feel these stones. To some, the words of the hymn come to mind, "Faith of our fathers! living still. . . ."

Cultural Enrichment

Alert teachers and parents are quick to make the most of "touch" objects from other countries. The gift of an Iona cross sent to a high schooler from Scotland initiated family study of that island. They read of St. Columba establishing a monastery there in 563 and of Iona becoming a Christian center from which missionaries were sent to Scotland and England. They learned of the restoration of buildings and community in the twentieth century and they plan for a trip to Iona to study and worship.

Teachers in a church in New Jersey anticipated the furlough of its denomination's missionaries from Thailand. The committee on Christian education decided that in the month preceding the visit the class sessions should be devoted to a study of Thailand and the church of Christ there.

The committee worked with the church school superintendent and teachers to collect books and pictures of Thai life and plan the teaching sessions. A church member who had lived in Thailand brought samples of clothing for both men and women, a miniature house and river boat, miniature tools and musical instruments, handwoven lunch baskets, straw trays and balls, umbrellas made of oiled paper and bamboo, hand-carved elephants of teak, dolls in national dress, and a road map of the country.

5
Tasting and Testing

One Maundy Thursday afternoon some travelers in Ohio looked for a church where they might attend evening service. As they drove along a ridge high above the Ohio River, they found a red brick, steepled church set against the hillside.

"Yes, we will have service tonight," the minister replied to their inquiry. "No, we will not have the Lord's Supper. On this night it is our custom to have an Upper Room Service in which children can partake of a supper with their families."

The travelers attended the service. The congregation gathered in the dining-social room of this rural church and sat at tables. Twelve men representing the disciples sat together around a table at the front of the room. Each "disciple" identified his role by telling how he had first met Jesus. Passages from Luke and John were read before the "supper" was served. Supper consisted of crackers, dried fruits, nuts, and fruit punch. Everyone ate in silence except for a few audible whispers of young children. Then each disciple read a Scripture selection giving one of the teachings of Jesus. Four young people sang "Go to Dark Gethsemane." Without another spoken word the congregation went upstairs to the sanctuary for a period of meditation and prayer. After the benediction they left in silence.

It is rather uncommon to find church leaders using the sense of taste in an educational way. But in this Upper Room Service the foods served helped the participants of all ages recall the physical conditions of the supper of Jesus and his friends. Certain passages of Scripture took on deeper meanings. Tasting was an important part of the service.

Perception Through Taste
It seems to adults as if a baby tries to put everything in his mouth.

PHILLIPS MEMORIAL
LIBRARY
PROVIDENCE, COLLEGE

And there is good reason. His taste buds are among the most sensitive organs he has early in life. Through his tongue he can learn about warm and cold, thick and thin, fuzzy and smooth, sticky, round, and other qualities. When he is old enough to attend church school his teachers notice that he will taste the paper, paste, play dough, toys—almost everything. He knows it is a good way for him to explore, test, and discover the things around him.

At regular snack time for three-, four-, and five-year-olds, teachers often change the flavors of cookies and juice, or may substitute a fruit or raw vegetable. Harvesttime is the season for tasting fullness of flavor. Grapes, apricots, peaches, melons, apples, papayas, celery, cauliflower buds, white turnip strips, crisp spinach, tiny new carrots, whatever grows best in a local area or garden, may be the flavor that can deepen a child's appreciation of God's plan for food to grow. Many of today's children know only the supermarket as the source of foods.

With a little ingenuity and originality the teacher can add to her church school resources some unusual things for tasting. One teacher asked a family traveling to Florida for a winter vacation to bring back a coconut for her class. None of the children had seen a coconut still in its outer husk. Getting into the coconut was a real chore. The teacher let the children do as much as they could. When the coconut was husked they pounded a large nail into it for draining the milk. Then they cracked the coconut open. With a knife the teacher carefully cut off the luscious white meat. That day at snack time the children truly enjoyed coconut as one of God's good gifts.

When a teacher had a winter vacation in the West Indies she carried back to her children a stalk of sugarcane. Being Northerners they did not know what it was, except for one child who thought it might be corn. But before telling them, she cut it and gave each child a piece to chew. They all sensed its sweetness, but many did not like it. However, their curiosity led them to ask questions when the teacher said that it was sugarcane from which sugar is made.

Children Appreciate Jewish Customs

In a weekday church nursery the teachers wanted the children to know of a custom observed by Jewish families in celebrating the Jewish New Year, or Rosh Hashanah. Pieces of apple and a bowl of honey were put on a table. When a child asked what these were for, a teacher sat

down and explained that this was the season of New Year for Jewish people. At this season, it is their custom to eat honey on apple and to say to each other, "May you have a happy New Year." Three of the children who were from Jewish homes were particularly interested. Honey on apple provided a new taste, and a pleasant one, for all who tried it. In fact, one of the boys requested honey on the apples he ate at home all that winter.

Some primary teachers have added tasting to their methods when the children have been studying Palestinian life and customs. They served dried fruits such as those used in Nazareth when Jesus was a boy: raisins, figs, and dates. And when available, they ate pomegranates and almonds. This can lead to additional learnings for children who live in climates where they have never seen these fruits grow. They ask many questions about the vines and trees and the process of drying.

As certain juniors asked questions about Jesus' last journey to Jerusalem they kept reiterating: "But *why* did Jesus go? Why was Passover so important that Jesus went to Jerusalem where his enemies were?" In response to questions the teachers and minister decided with the children to hold a "Passover feast" in their church school. They went to a rabbi for help.

It was an educational venture for the leaders as well as for the children. They studied the Passover event first and then the way in which faithful Jews remember in gratitude God's mighty act on their behalf. When they had their Passover service they tasted grated horseradish, a sweet, parsley dipped in salt water, matzoth, hard-cooked egg, and macaroons. Each morsel of food was symbolic and this was meaningful to the juniors. The extremes of taste from bitter to sweet helped them to feel something of the historical event. Young and old alike felt better acquainted with Jewish life and the reason for Jesus' celebration of the Passover. The study also gave new depth to the meaning of the Lord's Supper.

Even adults have wondered about the flavor of anise of which they read in the Bible in instructions concerning the tithing of spices. Yet every Christmas anise-flavored candy is among the popular hard candies of the season, and anise is the flavoring in Swedish limpa bread.

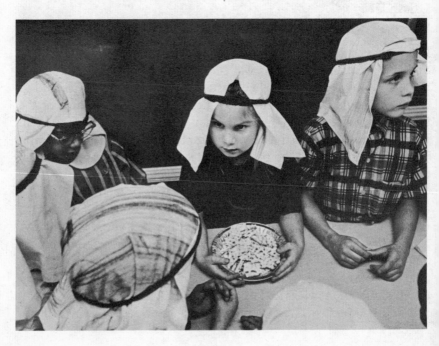

Foods of the World

An unusual experience of taste was reported [16] when a certain church celebrated Worldwide Communion by using the traditional breads from many countries. Women of the congregation baked the kinds of breads their mothers or grandmothers had baked from "old country" recipes. Seventeen loaves were brought to the church on the Sunday before and placed on the Communion table. A prayer of dedication followed. The loaves were kept fresh in a deepfreeze until the following Sunday when they were broken and pieces of each kind of bread were served on each plate. Romanian, Arabic, Hungarian, Chinese, Dutch, Swedish, German, English, Mexican, and others—breads of the world made the congregation feel truly a part of the large world family of man dependent on one God and Savior.

When a congregation had a family night series on India the high school students found a recipe for gajrelt, a sweet that is enjoyed in India. This sweet, made according to an American recipe, using grated carrot, condensed milk, butter, coconut, and raisins cooked to the right consistency, made a tasty candy. The women investigated Indian food, secured the necessary spices in advance, and made a curry for that family night. The foods aroused curiosity and created much discussion. The families were more ready to study India. Curry, tortilla, pilaf, and many other special foods have come to be favorites of people outside of the countries in which they originated. Enjoyment of foods of many nations makes for a kind of acquaintance and acceptance of one people by another. Even though it is surface knowledge, it is a beginning of understanding for some persons.

Several congregations concerned about hunger in the world hold an occasional luncheon on Sundays to eat a basic subsistence meal. The food may be rice and tea, or grits and coffee. Members go away hungry, of course, and have heard stories and seen pictures of persons who eat such a meal regularly. They pay a good price for this tasting venture and the proceeds go to the Church World Service hunger program.

Tasting and Teaching

It is a curious fact that the human memory associates some past incidents with likable flavors or foods. A woman of forty took one bite of a cracker at a friend's dinner party and exclaimed: "This is it! The cracker I have been wanting for years! This is what we had every morning in the first grade with our milk."

This basic fact of the association of past events with likable flavors or foods entered into the training of young school boys in the Palestinian synagogues of long ago. The rabbis gave them honey at school so that they would grasp the idea that learning is sweet.

Tasting, like other experiences, can be a positive or negative learning. When children experiment in tasting new foods they are conditioned by the reactions of the adults nearby. Teachers themselves need to experiment, enjoy, savor rather than take for granted the wonderful sense of taste. This will happen when they approach tasting with anticipation and curiosity, and leave it with gratitude and appreciation, even if the flavor is disliked.

Teachers will find that tasting is particularly helpful when used as a method with persons who are blind or deaf, or with any who have lost one of the other senses.

Curiosity can be stimulated through flavors: What is this food? How does it grow—on a tree, a plant, or as an underground root? Where does it come from—nearby or far away? Who might have planted it? Who prepared it? Who is the basic Source or Provider of all food?

When one looks for avenues of learning through the sense of taste, one can find many possibilities. Meaningful experiences of learning come from tasting.

6
Aromas to Be Caught

An American visitor to Guatemala found herself in the center of a Mayan Indian family religious ceremony on the day she visited the church of Santo Tomas. Broad circular steps led to the wide entrance to the church. On the bottom step a fire burned. As each individual or family approached this fire, they added to it from the bundle of wood they carried. Then a priest standing by the fire gave each worshiper a lighted stick of incense. Some prayed on each step, believing that the smoke of their incense would take their prayers directly to heaven. Others moved slowly up the steps to the interior of the church.

Inside the church many candles were burning and a sweet odor filled the sanctuary. There were no seats. Many families sat in circles on the floor, burning their bundles of flower petals as they prayed for health, food, and forgiveness. The atmosphere was heavy, but a sense of religious devotion pervaded the church. The religious practices of these Mayan Indians are influenced by racial memories. Although such practices may formerly have been related to idols, their current usage is adapted to the people's new faith, Christianity.

Old Testament Incense

The use of incense formed a part of the religious ceremonies of many ancient nations. Its use was taken over by the Hebrews of Old Testament times from the Canaanite religion. The Hebrew word for "sweet spices" has its root in the word meaning "to smell."

In Ex. 30:7–8 we read of the use of incense every morning and evening, "a perpetual incense before the LORD throughout your generations." The ingredients required for the incense are described in detail in vs. 22–25, 34–35. The Hebrews associated their worship experiences in the tabernacle and in the Temple with fragrance. To this day, in many countries, synagogues and churches use incense regularly in congregational worship.

Associations with the Sense of Smell

Everyone can recall positive influences of different odors. From happy childhood experiences many adults remember the smell of new-mown hay, of ocean air, of a campfire. Others recall the fragrance of a honeysuckle hedge, of a border of roses or lilacs, of a patch of wild mint. Howard Thurman once said that when everything is pulled out, when everything seems to be gone, there is always the smell of fresh earth, new fallen rain, and freshly cut grass.

The father of a nine-year-old boy had been away from home two weeks on a business trip. One day the boy happened to be near the open clothes closet in his parents' bedroom. He sniffed. Then he grabbed his father's clothes to him and said: "M-m-m, my Daddy. This smells like my Daddy." His mother did not smell it, but the lonesome boy did.

The scent of lighted candles is especially noticeable at the Christmas Eve service when a church has dozens of candles burning. The fragrance takes the older members back to childhood services of worship. A woman whose church uses candles every Sunday associates their smell with prayer; she instinctively prays when she smells candles burning. This is also true in her home, when candles are lighted and grace is said at dinner. Children may have a similar feeling of reverence, remembering the glow and fragrance of candles in a church school service of worship.

Two distinct fragrances have come to be associated today with two holy days of the Christian church. The woodsy, pungent smell of the fir tree brought into the church at Advent time foretells Christmas, and the sweet heaviness of the lily, used as a symbol of purity, denotes Easter. These two scents are so closely associated with the church that, even in hot summertime, a person in the woods may refer to a whiff of the fragrance of an evergreen tree by saying, "Just smell those Christmas trees!" The regal lily that blooms in August gardens is commonly spoken of as an "Easter lily."

One January a weekday nursery class had a blooming hyacinth on their windowsill. A boy stopped riding his truck long enough to smell of the flower. With a broad smile he looked up at the teacher and said, "That smells like Easter." She was amazed and pondered on this a long time. The association of scent to recall a certain day was strong in this young boy who had only lived through three Easters in his brief lifetime.

The spicy fragrance of fir and pine is usually associated with the family Christmas tree, but it can also be related to church experiences when children decorate their rooms with branches and take part in an Advent celebration such as described in Chapter 1.

Aromas of Other Lands

A foresighted teacher in the church had the privilege of taking a trip around the world. Everywhere she went she wondered how she might best take back to her pupils and friends a true feeling for the peoples of different countries. She took snapshots and recorded incidents. She purchased representative pieces of the arts in each land, thinking of both their appearance and their fragrance. She consciously looked for items that carried with them a pleasing aroma.

In Lebanon she found a small donkey cut from the famous cedars of Lebanon (Ps. 92:12), and in Jordan a carved box with a faint smell of olive wood. It was the musty smell of teakwood that attracted her in Thailand, and she bought an elephant carved out of teakwood by a person being treated for leprosy. Tea from Taiwan included the smoke-flavored Lapsang souchong and the sweet jasmine. She was delighted to find a sandalwood fan in Japan. As a little girl she had often smelled Great-aunt Laura's fan with mystical delight. At last she could own such a fan herself and let many children in her church know something of the Orient through its intriguing spiciness. Inasmuch as inexpensive imported objects are now for sale everywhere, other church school teachers can readily find articles with an aroma that will help develop appreciation of people in other parts of the world.

Odors Give Warnings and Invitations

The Kodiak bear is a vicious animal of the north with a seventeen-inch paw print and twelve-foot standing reach on a tree. When Roger Caras, naturalist and author, spoke about the Kodiak he said, "His eyes make him suspicious, his ears make him suspicious, but his nose tells him."

This is not necessarily true for people, but the human nose does alert persons and give them warnings. When one smells gas he is warned of a dangerous leakage and when he smells smoke he is cautioned of fire. The odor of fresh paint makes him watch where he walks and what he touches. Or the aroma of baking bread will call one to a task in the kitchen. A blind student can tell when he approaches the art room in high school by the smell of oil paints that seeps into the hall. He knows the woodworking shop by the smell of freshly cut wood and shavings.

Some teachers use the sense of smell as an invitation to a pleasant learning situation. One junior department superintendent has an electric coffeepot steaming when her teachers come at eight thirty on Sunday mornings. Hot cocoa is available for the boys and girls, some of whom leave home without breakfast. The enticing aroma that welcomes all who approach the room helps create a pleasant atmosphere for learning experiences that follow.

A certain primary teacher discovered that when her class meets at the church during the week for special projects, the whole atmosphere is set by the odor of hot popcorn jumping in an electric popper. The smell and the taste of popcorn give the children a respite after their day at school. Soon they are ready to turn to more serious pursuits.

Teachers Plan

The sense of smell is as truly a vehicle for learning as the senses of touch, sight, taste, and hearing. Smelling is closely allied to tasting. The olfactory nerves provide more flavors than the taste buds of the tongue. Most tasting depends upon smelling which refines flavors. Tasting and smelling are considered so important in the commercial world that artificial flavors and aromatics are manufactured and have wide sale. For example, the smoky flavor of meat now comes from a bottle and the smell of a new car comes from a spray can.

Often the teacher has to sensitize children to their olfactory sense and make them aware of it as one of God's gifts. Taking time to sniff and whiff and to inhale deeply are ways the teacher makes a child aware. He points out the fragrance of the soap in the washroom, of cinnamon cookies at snack time, of narcissus blooms on the windowsill. Sometimes he makes a game of smelling by hiding one object in a paper bag— an onion, a banana, a piece of chocolate, a bit of perfume on a handkerchief—for them to identify by smell only. The children take turns, trying to guess what they smell in the bag. When children are outdoors for a walk or playtime, they often can identify delightful and strange smells in the atmosphere.

One November the children and teachers in a primary department planned a Thanksgiving gift of apples for the three adults who were the staff of their church: minister, sexton, secretary. Knowing that one can give more readily and happily if he first possesses, the teachers provided pieces of apple to be eaten as a snack. Yellow and red apples, bronze and golden, they tried them all. But the teacher had to point out the fragrance of the apples and the variation between different kinds.

On the next two Sundays as their gift apples were accumulating, the children would go to the basket and smell and smell and smell.

Another fragrant gift was that made by a cabin of girls and their leader in a summer camp. The director's birthday was approaching and they wanted to express their affection. So they made a necklace of flowers, like a Hawaiian lei. They gathered red clover blossoms along the roadside, cut off the stems, and strung the flower heads on a string like beads. They presented their lei at dinner and the director said: "The necklace is delightful! I feel as if I am wearing clover perfume."

Negative Reactions as Well as Positive

The sense of smell does arouse emotions, but sometimes they are negative. The odor of a musty room in an old house or of a cold, dank

cave impels a person to turn away. And some odors turn children away from the church.

One child was repelled by the smell of the locker room of a church swimming pool. One day, while walking past the building, he said disdainfully, "That church stinks." It was hard to persuade him to go to that church again. Another boy did not want to go to his church because of the stuffy, close atmosphere in the room where his class met on Sunday. Such odors, of which the teacher is not always aware, are a hindrance to learning. Good fresh air in any teaching or worship area should have high priority. The smell of a room or the deadness of the air may counteract the positive effect of interesting materials and of even the engaging personality of the teacher.

An odor that attracts children enriches the teacher's lesson plan. Subconsciously fragrance, as well as the lack of offensive scents, adds pleasantness to one's early memories of church school experiences. Later in life, at most unlikely times and in most unlikely places, an adult may recall with gratitude a religious experience of his youth because of its association with a pleasant smell.

7
Doing Is Learning: Creative Hands, Creative Movement

Like a sharp warning bell the child's comment alerted every teacher in the room on that autumn Sunday morning. The children had been getting acquainted by talking about the members of their families. Then they began to draw pictures of their homes and families on large sheets of paper. One little girl watched and squirmed, picked up a crayon and put it down. Finally, she handed her crayon to a teacher and said: "You draw it for me. I can't. My mommy has showed me so many times I haven't learned it for myself."

With questions and conversation, she was encouraged patiently. She tried it for herself that day and in many successive weeks, for none of the teachers would draw on her paper. They knew what the child herself implied—that if she was to learn, she would have to do it herself. Her ideas would have to be expressed in her own manner and at her own speed. No one can learn for someone else.

Growing Through Creative Expression

How wisely the Chinese proverb states it:

> I hear and I forget,
> I see and I remember,
> I do and I understand.

Reaching out to the world through the five senses helps a person to perceive in different ways and to different degrees. Meanings take shape in his mind and concepts are built. But experiences of seeing, hearing, feeling, tasting, and smelling are strengthened by experiences of expressing oneself. A person learns by doing. In order to tie a knot, set up a tent, paddle a canoe, use a typewriter, milk a cow, he actually has to set about doing it many times in order to learn or achieve. Hearing lectures, seeing pictures, reading books, watching demonstrations, all help, but he has not learned until he himself does it.

Creative expression develops the intellect: it involves choices and decisions, the solving of problems, dealing with various materials, and exposing inner feelings or ideas. From past meanings come new ones; as the learner classifies his thinking, sees new relationships, differentiates and generalizes ideas when he tries to communicate through his act of doing. For example, turn back to Chapter 1 for the brief description of how a growing child's concept of the church might have developed. Note how his ideas were clarified and changed with perceptual or sensory experiences and how different meanings could envolve when he built a church of blocks, drew a picture of a church, took a trip to the organ, and to the minister's study. Doing these things, and others, for many Sundays gave added depth of understanding to his growing concept of the church. More advanced experiences in grade school years will enlarge the concept; more involved expression or doing will refine it.

Teachers are not to be misled by the phrase "doing is learning." Not all doing is positive learning just because it happens within the confines of church walls or within the loving community of church people. Some doing is sheer busywork: the unimaginative repetition of coloring with crayons in church school has dismayed and bored many a child. Worse yet is when he has to color outline pictures, or copy patterns, or trace figures. These things induce him to conform to the teacher's ideas. Even a sample shown by the teacher confines a pupil's thinking. One Sunday a primary teacher showed her class a picture she had drawn of the Israelites in the wilderness when manna and quail were sent to them. The "freehand" drawings of her children that morning were all influenced by her picture and partially copied it! There was no fully creative thinking and doing. One of the best ways to help children achieve self-direction for facing the unknown future is to help them be original, venturesome, and independent in their expressional activity.

Creative expression as used in this chapter may be of two types: making something with one's hands and expression through movement and action of the whole body. Both involve thinking and both develop best from a fullness of mind and heart. This "fullness" is what the teacher plans before expecting expression unless she seeks to know the child's hidden agenda (what he brings in his mind and emotions from home).

A primary teacher in Ohio who knew the value of creative work with hands usually planned her Sunday schedule to include it. She developed a session through conversation, story, pictures, and Bible-reading. Then she gave the children a challenge for creative expression. She allowed time to think and feel as they talked about the Scripture, time to plan what they would make, time to carry out the plan, and finally time to appreciate and evaluate. Whether it was individual or group work, the teacher included each step. The children chose to make things other than those she had in mind, but she was ready and eager for this. The basic steps—think, feel, plan, carry out, appreciate, and evaluate—were needed in any case.

One Sunday in this primary group the conversation was directed toward discovery of how the ten lepers and the people nearby must have felt at the time Jesus cured the sick men. What might they have said and done? Two children used hand puppets from the cupboard as they pretended they were two men who had observed the event and had gone home to tell what they had seen. Their conversation in these roles was perceptive. Others wanted to paint pictures of the healed men as they went home to tell their families. And a girl made a clay figure of the one man who returned to thank Jesus. Because all of these expressions demanded thinking from each child as he was "doing," it is more certain that there was depth in the learning process. It is entirely possible that each child took home from church a better understanding of the response of persons to Jesus and his ministry.

Creative Hands

Making Things. Although most church school teachers recognize the need for learners to make things with their hands, many expect a "good" finished product—and a "good" product in their minds must have perfectionism and realism. "I want my pupils to do exact work and have it look like something," said a teacher. This indicates also that such teachers are more concerned with the result than the process. But the process is where the learning occurs. These teachers are missing the fun of teaching! They have not yet learned to enjoy the uniqueness and child-like freshness of individual work at every age and stage of growing. Nor do they know how to stimulate, then stand back and relish that wonderful inner process which evolves creative work and adds to mental achievement.

The pleasure of making things with their hands is not limited to children. Teen-agers and adults need to express what they learn in the church too. If they have done creative work before, they will do skillful and imaginative work when older. If they have not made things as children in the church, they will need encouragement and inspiration. Even adults could profit from some of the following experiences enjoyed by the young.

Before Christmas a class of older juniors decided early in December to decorate their department Christmas tree with Christian symbols as ornaments. The idea came to them in the midst of their study on church history. A child chose a symbol and drew the design on a cardboard or plastic lid (from cottage cheese and other dairy products). Then the design was covered with glue, and glitter was laid on heavily. Some ornaments were made out of aluminum-foil tart pans, with edges cut like flower petals to catch light rays. The symbol, made of glitter, was placed in the base of a wee pie pan. There was a variety of designs: ship, dove, fish, cock, and the triquetra for the Trinity. But one in particular caught the attention of the whole class. It was four geese heads with open, cackling bills, a symbol to remind early Christians not to talk in the service of worship. In another church where juniors made symbols into tree ornaments, they used sheets of very heavy plastic (from an art store) to cut various shapes and make the symbol with glitter. Each child made as many as he wanted for his own family's tree. One little girl made all symbols of peace for her tree!

Young people in junior high who studied the origin of symbols in the setting of the early church chose to reproduce some as mosaic glass tiles. Each chose the symbol he wished to put into a tile. He drew his design the proper size to look well in a 9″ x 9″ space, then transferred the symbol to a vinyl tile that would be its backing. He experimented with the varicolored bits of glass on his design to determine what colors he preferred and how the pieces would fit the design. Then he glued the glass bits on to the vinyl base. Next came experimentation with colors for the background and the gluing of those pieces. The last step was the most difficult—the wedging of the grout into all the wee crevices and the wiping clean of the excess, which must be meticuously done over and over again. It was interesting to the teacher to notice how the students helped one another in this process. When finished, the tiles were exhibited in the church social room so that the entire fellowship could enjoy them and ask questions.

Some eleventh- and twelfth-graders who found church history interesting were particularly intrigued with the life of Martin Luther. They decided to make colored slides and write a script depicting his life and influence on the church. To make the slides they drew pictures on onionskin with different-colored ballpoint pens. The 2" x 2" slide is a very small space in which to work, but it was a challenge to these young people. When each picture was finished it was fastened into a regular cardboard slide mount (available at camera shops). They kept a projector in their room during the work period so they could see each slide as it was finished. This gave encouragement and stimulus to all the workers. This is the kind of work that would appeal to adults in depicting the history of their own church for one year, such as a report for the annual meeting.

Besides the practical sewing of garments and hospital supplies that women do in most churches, a few groups have found decorative banners to be their choice. The social hall of bare cement blocks looked too barren to the women in a new church building so they made interesting banners about 4' x 16' to add warmth to the walls. Some were abstract designs, resembling collage work, some symbolic and meticulous; all carried meanings for the maker and her church—and the colors were a sensory joy!

Women in another church sewed a dossal, or large banner, to hang over the altar of their church. It was made of various fabrics, with the designs appliqued in different embroidery stitches. The design itself was the work of children in the church school who drew pictures of selected Bible stories and arranged them on a dossal-shaped paper: Adam and Eve, Noah's ark, Moses in the bulrushes, Jesus' birth and baptism. This was reproduced on fabric. Sensory learning and enjoyment for both children and adults will continue as long as their dossal is used.

Radiant banners of felt were made to add joy and focus to a series of meetings in a city church in which the committee was directing the thinking of its members to "service where I am" in the city; if a realtor, get into public housing; if a teacher, give your best to solving school problems that cause strikes. These banners were 3′ x 8′ in size, gay in their colors, artistically casual in their letters which were glued to the background. They bore such insights as: "Thank God for the City," "Do your own thing," "Joy, Joy, Joy" after the style of Sister Corita's serigraphs. The committee hung them from the balcony railing of their dark church and they were stimulants to the people in the pews who wrestled together on how to be Christian today in their city.

Eight symbolic and exquisite banners depicting eight of the nine statements of faith in *The Constitution of The United Presbyterian Church in the United States of America, Part I, Book of Confessions*, were designed by a minister and choir director in New York State. The women of the church made them carefully and beautifully of different fabrics. They were planned to help the congregation understand that although the faith of the church in Jesus Christ stays the same, each new era has particular concerns such as those reflected in the latest Confession of 1967. Used first in a service of worship with a trumpet and drum processional, then loaned to other churches who wished to borrow them, the banners now hang against the sanctuary wall where they continually stimulate perceptual learning. A second set of banners was made and it travels all over the country. Requests have far exceeded availability so the women have cut patterns to size 3′2″ x 6′5″) for each banner and they may be purchased in packets.[17] Much research went into designing the banners, choosing materials, and planning the service of worship.

Family Stimulation. It is interesting to notice how much some parents value creative work for their children. They encourage it by providing the raw materials at home, planning a space for working, appreciating what is done, and sometimes suggesting something to do.

It was Beth's mother, of course, who thought of finger painting in the bathtub. They lived in an apartment so small for such a messy fun-thing-to-do that the best solution was a rubber suction mat in the tub for her two-year-old and then plenty of bright colored paint. She covers herself as well as the tub; when liquid soap is added she washes both. The mother gets as much pleasure as little Beth!

When an adult friend was ill, parents suggested to their sons that a get-well card might be appreciated. This did not mean a card from the store—the suggestion indicated to the boys that they make cards. The eight-year-old-boy had fished with this friend the previous summer, so he drew a fisherman pulling in a fish that said, "Get well soon." The youngest could only make lines—pretty colored lines with Magic Markers—but they too carried love to a friend. The third boy wrote a rhyme and on the back put his own copyright sign, "a Mark Original" inside of a crown.

When grown-ups are extra busy around home at Christmastime, art materials are a release to visiting grandchildren. It is amazing what can be done with crayons when a child is free to think and express by herself. Ten-year-old Carole drew her idea of the Annunciation. In the drawing the angel stands at the rear, having just announced to Mary that she has been chosen to bear the Son of God. Mary responds: she jumps in midair, arms and legs outstretched, hair blowing as she replies, "Wow!" Needless to say, Carole's grandparents framed the drawing and hung it in their living room.

Working with clay developed into a winter hobby for the whole family one year because mother was taking lessons in ceramics. Not only were some interesting objects made, especially by the twelve-year-old son, but the greatest value came from the pleasure of molding clay in one's hands with quieting music played on the radio. It affected them all the same way: clay aborbed tension and weariness.

A Group Project. In one church a class of twenty juniors is taught by three teachers who work as a team. As they plan in advance they decide who will assume the leadership and how the others will assist in each part of the session. One morning the lead teacher told the story of Pentecost (Acts 1:1-5; ch. 2) and asked thought-provoking questions for clarification and review. Then she began to sing the first stanza of "The Church Is Wherever God's People Are Praising"[18] and the children joined her.

Another teacher in the team asked, "What was the most important part of the story for people who became members of his church that day?"

Some answered "Seeing people from many nations" and "Hearing Peter speak." But three children replied immediately, "They knew Jesus was the Son of God."

"How can we tell this story of Pentecost on a big mural for our walls so we will think about it often? What scenes of the story can we paint?" the teacher asked the children.

She guided the discussion as the children decided on scenes:

1. The disciples talking and praying in the upper room;

2. The discussion in the streets where crowds had gathered for the Feast of Pentecost—with Peter preaching;

3. Some of the crowd being baptized.

Each child chose the part of the story he wanted to work on. Three large sheets of wrapping paper (3' x 8') were placed on the floor, and each teacher led a group in planning what they would put in their scene. The children lightly sketched in their ideas with chalk before painting. As the groups worked, the teachers watched and answered questions, making sure each child had a part in creating the scene.

When the work was almost finished, one of the teachers sang softly near her group, "The church is wherever . . . ." Later this music was played on the piano as an indication to the children that they were to finish and gather for worship. Everything these boys and girls had done helped to prepare them for worship:

> they had heard a well-told story;
> they had practiced a song;
> they had talked about both;
> they had planned to illustrate the story;
> they had painted three scenes for a mural.

This was not handwork or busywork but "thinking" and "making" that led them to respond to God in worship even as the people had done at Pentecost.

Making Music. Probably the music of a rattle is the very first made by young hands. Rhythm instruments follow soon thereafter, either at home or at church school. The sounds of rhythm sticks, triangles, wrist bells, sand blocks, drums, cymbals, all add delight and rhythmical learning to the young child. When the teacher uses an autoharp or guitar the children even try those instruments. Both are effective with the current religious folk songs. The recorder is an inexpensive instrument and fairly simple to play for children or youth. It is used effectively as a "shepherd's flute" at Christmastime, but is useful for hymn practice since only the melody is played. Listening teachers sometimes hear an original melody or a song and can encourage that child to complete his creation.

A primary teacher in a vacation school often sang softly and half to herself as she moved from group to group in the work centers. She sang or hummed a new song that the group was learning so that it might be absorbed. One day she heard two girls singsong the words of Peter (Matt. 16:13–20) that they had just heard in a story. As they painted on a mural they kept repeating these words in rhythm, "Jesus is the Son of the living God." The teacher commented that they might be able to make up a tune to go with the words. Others in the group joined the challenge. As the painting progressed, many individual tunes were heard. Finally, they took time to listen to each other's songs and the group decided that they liked Allison's tune best. "I'll write the music," said the teacher, "then I'll play it on the piano so all of us can learn it." It became their own song and they sang it often with great satisfaction.

Handwork May Be Feedback. A second-grade teacher believes that things made with hands may be excellent channels for "feedback"; that is, they provide another way of quizzing on what has been taught, of clarifying and reviewing ideas and attitudes. One Sunday after the children had been thinking together for several months through hymns, pictures, Scripture-reading, and conversation, she said, "By using any materials on the table, how could you show that 'God is love'?"

This was a more general idea than she had ever given them. But her children were used to creative work and she wondered how they would express this basic quality of God. Quietly she watched. A girl chose paints and did a symbolic picture. In the center she painted a red heart (symbol of love to a child) and on either side the sun and the moon. This was her way of showing that God's love is in the midst of the space world, not limited to her, her family, or even her country. Others used clay, colored chalk, and charcoal to make representations of family, friends, and Jesus.

The teacher whose junior high class made mosaic Christian symbols (mentioned earlier) greeted them on Sunday with paper and pencils. "Before we continue our work on symbols," he said, "Let's do some writing on these two questions: Why did I choose this symbol? What did it mean in the early life of the church?" and he wrote his questions on the chalkboard. This was a time for personal meditation and the sorting of ideas. Discussion came at the end of the session after the teacher had had time to read the answers during the class's creative work. Misconceptions of symbols in the church were corrected and concepts deepened by helping each other think through meanings.

An art teacher in a parochial school invited her students to select an incident from Jesus' life and make a painting of it. As the children worked she noticed that a girl was painting the crucifixion and there was a definite smile on the face of Jesus. This puzzled the teacher but she refrained from questioning. When the painting was finished the girl asked the teacher to look at it. Then the child asked: "Did you notice that Jesus is smiling? He's smiling because he's made it possible for all of us to be forgiven."

A mother and father arrived at their church gingerly carrying a large carton. They asked to see the kindergarten superintendent alone and showed her a Lego (interlocking building rods) construction inside the box. Their five-year-old boy had made it at home all by himself. It was his church. He had remembered many details: lobby and elevator to kindergarten room, the room for three-year-olds where his sister goes, the sanctuary with cross, lectern, Communion table, pulpit, organ, and pews. "We just want you to know that your teaching is not in vain. We realize that one does not always know just what a young child is learning, but this shows something of what John has received from you."

Creative Movement

Rhythmic Movement. Creative rhythmic movement is the expression of what a child is thinking and feeling through the actions of his body, without any speaking. In it one does not have to master the skill of using a paintbrush or tool of any kind, he simply expresses himself through total action or movement.

Visualize the pleasurable learning that took place when eighteen Illinois juniors, dressed in gold gowns of corded cotton, interpreted the Creation through rhythmic movement. The process by which this was achieved was carefully planned. The teacher of juniors who could lead rhythmic movement discussed the first chapter of Genesis with the director of Christian education. Together they looked for theological meanings and how they would be interpreted. Later the teacher introduced the passage to the juniors by reading it beautifully, by asking them questions, by letting them ask questions. They became thoroughly acquainted with it. Next they heard the director read the Genesis story to music so they could feel the beauty and rhythm of the word pictures. Finally the teacher looked at the boys and girls and said: "If you were to tell this beautiful story without using any words, how would you do it? Let's stand in a large circle and as I tell the story each of you show how you would do it with movement." Each did his own and saw what others did. One girl wanted to imitate another for a specific movement because hers was particularly expressive. They continued to experiment until they found the movements they liked best. For the creations on separate days, small groups would take part. For the refrain, "And God saw that it was good," they all took part. Then in unity they expressed the story through movement. Each had contributed something to the total. It was helpful to them as individuals and it was a sensory experience for others in their departmental worship.

Creative Dramatics. Creative dramatics requires body movement and usually spontaneous speaking. Begun simply with three- or four-year-olds it may at first be a responsive action to a teacher's song or story done as a group rather than as individual parts. But each child feels it is individual, nonetheless. Four-year-old Matthew was slow to take part in such pantomime, but one spring morning he joined the others in being a seed that would waken with sun and rain as the teacher sang. The children named the kinds of seeds they were and tried to control growing muscles to show how gradually they could "grow." After this dramatic play they planted wheat seeds in their window box. When Matthew's mother lingered after school to talk, the teacher suggested that he tell her about planting seeds. Matthew stood still, looked at the teacher in a bewildered way, and finally replied, "I *were* a seed." The important thing for him that morning was not planting seeds with his hands but being a seed with his whole body.

First-graders dramatized the long story they had heard of the brothers going to Egypt to get grain and having to return for Benjamin. They made four scenes of it and kept the whole in mind because the teacher told parts of the story and they did the conversation. When fifth-graders dramatized the exodus one boy was a severe Pharaoh, some girls delighted in being the plagues that bothered him, many chose to be the escaping Israelites. Four boys refused to take part. When the teacher asked if they would be the Red Sea they willingly accepted and gave the motions of great waters rolling back.

Role-playing. The taking of roles to act the viewpoint or person of someone else is another type of learning that involves the total person. Sometimes this happens informally as in nursery school or kindergarten when children are busy in work centers. When either boy or girl care for a doll in the "house center" they are acting the roles of father and mother. The teacher does not tell them what to do, she observes what they do and listens to what they say. "You bad, bad doll," said Todd. "Now you sit in that corner till I tell you to get up," and with a dominant stance he was off to other work. Tom learns the role of a man at home and practices it at school.

Role-playing for older children and adults is usually guided by the leader. A problem situation is described and possible solutions discussed briefly from all sides. The characters take different viewpoints and there is at least one unpopular or difficult role. The leader asks persons to volunteer for each particular role and to take a part contrary to their own nature and beliefs, if at all possible. In this way difficult real-life situations can be examined and explored more freely because the observers know that when the roles are being played, persons are not giving their own opinions. Thus free discussion of the problem from many angles is opened up. To accomplish this end the leader must cut off the acting at an appropriate time and in the evaluation of it always refer to "the role Ted Brown was playing" or "Jane Smith's role showed us . . . ." Participants can then make private plans for testing new insights and practicing newfound behavior. Probably this kind of expression is not used frequently enough in church education where we are concerned with understanding one another and maintaining healthful relationships within controversy as well as agreement. This way of learning would help youth and adults discuss community problems of rights, real estate, teen-age limits, adult rigidity, church procedures, and many more.

Role-playing can also be used to interpret Biblical situations. The difference between it and dramatization is that the "lines" are never frozen. Every time a group plays out a situation the participants vary what they say. An excellent example of this took place in a Lenten experience for juniors with a discerning teacher. In this Manhattan church it is customary to have a family service of worship on Good Friday at five thirty in the evening, planned and directed by juniors, junior highs, and senior highs. The leaders of these groups chose the theme: "Why Good Friday? Why did Jesus have to die?" The teacher acting as chairman for the plan thoroughly studied the records of Matthew, Mark, and Luke and wrote in her own words answers to the theme questions from the viewpoints of: the religious leaders of that day; the disciples; Jesus himself. Her paper was discussed by the teachers involved for their own background information, but it was not read with the children or youth who volunteered to work on this service outside of church school time. At their first session the leader asked them questions related to the background events to see how much they knew and understood. Then she led them in finding answers they did not know by looking in the Gospels. They talked about the religious leaders at length: what their job was as they saw it (the teacher described some of their petty laws), how they carried it out, why they did not like Jesus, specific questions to him, how they must have felt to be challenged by this man. They figured out that all the leaders would not feel the same toward Jesus, that some would be more hateful and at least one might still be of inquiring mind. Similarly they ferreted out what was happening to the disciples in those days and how they must have felt as individuals. Then they read the portions on Jesus and why he took the stand he did.

After two sessions of exciting study in which the children had searched for their own answers in the Gospels and for the feelings of persons within their own feelings, the teacher gave a situation for role-playing. The setting was the office of the high priest, Caiphas, who was president of the religious leaders, the Sanhedrin. The roles would be those of high priest and many religious leaders discussing the man Jesus who was stirring up trouble in the land. The difficult role would be that of one leader who did not go along with the others—he was still pondering Jesus' way and their ways. When the roles were taken each boy and girl spoke freely and originally from the background of his study. The boy who had the difficult role asked many "why" questions and finally said, "I can't agree with you. I can't go along with what you want to do so I'll have no part in it," and he walked out of the office. These juniors played this role several times and no one person ever gave the same speech or line of reasoning. If one took a certain attitude, then another became a different leader. In the final presentation, the leader who would "have no part in it" was a different boy than had done that in rehearsals. This showed that they all knew the basic ideas to be discussed and they all could play any role. The same was true of the section on the disciples. Palestinian headgear was the only costuming.

For the third part, "Jesus speaks," a boy and a girl read quotations from the Gospels and they were recorded on tape. These three parts, two of role-playing Scripture and one of reading it, were called vignettes, and presented "The Word" in the Good Friday service.

The counterpart to the vignettes of the juniors was that presented by the teen-agers as their present-day response to each part of the Word. The junior highs wrote poems and free verse reacting to the reasoning of the religious leaders and the feelings of the disciples. The senior highs did creative rhythmical movements and role situations to express how they could be true to God's message through Jesus of how he wants his creatures to live together. They projected real issues to the congregation in moving, effective ways.

This Good Friday service of worship was so planned and arranged that involvement was required of the congregation as well as all the participants. One could not just sit and listen; to hear or not to hear. With the progression of the prelude, Marcel Dupré's "Crucifixion" from the *Symphonie Passion,* one saw appropriate colored slides of the trial of Jesus. The hymns, "O Sacred Head Now Wounded" and "Were You There When They Crucified My Lord?" caught up one's thinking and prepared for the Word in the vignettes, poems, roles, and rhythmical movements. The closing litany of confession and dedication led one through suffering to inconquerable love: "Love lives forever! Praise be to God! Amen." It was natural and meaningful to think "Love" immediately when handed a white daisy at the door by the senior high youth who had taken part. Perceptual learnings of many kinds made up this service of worship.

Teachers, Too, Must Become Creative

We cannot expect children and youth to be free and creative in the expression of what they are learning unless their teachers are free and

imaginative. Sometimes it is difficult for leaders to grasp the importance
of creative work with hands. One of the best ways for them to come to
such understanding is to make things themselves. At a leadership education weekend an artist admitted that he had never painted religious
ideas nor thought of his class as doing such. A third-grade teacher had
never used clay and a school supervisor had never tried anything with
her hands. Each in his own church was teaching in the old ways of
reading verses around the circle, giving reports, filling in outline maps.
But after experimenting with clay, paints, puppets, stained-glass and
collage materials to express what they had studied that weekend on
"the Bible" they could see that teachers, too, must learn to create with
hands. At that same weekend these teachers had the opportunity to
express the incident of the commandments and the golden calf in creative rhythmical movement accompanied by old Israeli music.

Such "doing" for the learning of teachers can be done in each church or in clusters of churches. Only in the *act of doing* does one discover that the process is more important than the product. It is in the *process* that the learning takes place. Having had their own experiences in creative expression, adults become more sensitive teachers and more well-rounded persons.

8
Words, Written Words

Most teaching and learning are dependent on language, and we take for granted a facility with words. They are the symbols that give meaning to the world around us. They are the means by which we think God's thoughts after him. Yet, literacy is a relative thing and we learn to express ourselves in writing only by writing.

In the burst of the current knowledge explosion, religious men recognize God at work as he opens vast, potential discoveries to man. Whether in church, school, or home this special God-given gift of language for thinking, speaking, and writing must be encouraged and stimulated. Creative thinking can clarify and advance human thought. Creative writing preserves it, and stimulates productive thinking. God speaks today through words of man even as he has spoken through the centuries.

Writing Serves Many Purposes

There are many reasons for writing and many purposes for which it can be used in church education. One winter eight-year-old Anne attended a series of family night programs, six Sunday evenings, at the church with her family. The subject was mission study on the problems of migrant workers. The committee in charge decided that for the last program all the classes would meet together to share their findings. They would have a panel with representatives from each class. One of the committee telephoned Anne and asked if she would represent the primary department on the panel. She said she would have to think it over. After half an hour in her room she went to her mother and said: "I've decided to do it. I got more yeses than noes."

Anne told her mother that many reasons had come to mind for doing it and for not doing it, so she wrote them on paper. She had one column for "Yes, I'll do it" and another for "No, I can't do it," one of which was, "I don't know enough about migraines." The act of writing the reasons helped Anne to sort out the confusion of ideas that rushed to her mind.

Such a process of clarifying thoughts has been used by many church school classes. A group of juniors sorted out their varying opinions in regard to their celebration of Halloween, in deciding whether they would have a party or collect for UNICEF. By writing the pros and the cons for each, they arrived at a satisfactory group decision.

A senior high department went through the same process in deciding which day of the week they would meet at the church for study and service projects. They attend morning worship on Sundays and wanted another day for their study and activities.

Some teachers have found that on occasion copying information helps to fix it in the minds of students. For this reason a third-grade teacher had her children write the Shema on a scroll; this helped them memorize Deut. 6:4-5.

A teacher of adults surprised the class one Sunday morning by passing out paper and pencils. During the session he asked the men and women to write the Apostles' Creed. It might have been expected that all could do it because they declare their faith each Sunday by repeating the Creed together in morning worship. Yet only 2 percent of the class could write it in its entirety, which showed that when they recited it on Sundays they depended upon the leadership of the minister to carry them along. The teacher was checking on "memory work" because the adults had criticized the children and young people for not memorizing more Scripture and hymns.

Writing may be used for checking one's knowledge, as is done in a written test. Writing what one knows is personal; each person has to answer for himself. When the teacher looks at the papers he can see how well the desired facts are understood or known. He may give a true-false test or a multiple-choice test. In both the learner chooses an answer. The important discussion that follows such tests helps each to know whether he had the correct answers and if not, why. Misconceptions are corrected.

Another kind of written test is one in which the students write a phrase or a few sentences in answering questions. This kind of test is sometimes best for bringing to light haziness about facts. A brief test of this type is the following one used by a junior teacher: the answers are those given by a ten-year-old boy.

Picture study of *The Adoration of the Shepherds* (detail) by Giorgione:

1. Has the artist made anyone the center of attention in this picture? "Yes."
2. How has he done this? "Everyone is looking at the kid."
3. Why? "Because he is Jesus."
4. Why are the shepherds kneeling? "Because he is the king."
5. What do you like about this picture? "Good art."

Besides checking knowledge of facts a written test may reveal attitudes. No one right answer is expected or even possible on such a test. For example, knowing that junior highs are generally rebellious and ask questions about the value of "doing things the old way," one teacher planned to have his pupils do some writing on the day they studied about the cleansing of the Temple. They discovered in reading John 2:13-22 that Jesus violently overthrew the "old way" of doing business in the Temple. After discussing the terms "Passover," "sacrifice of animals," "Temple," and "money changers" to get background information, the teacher asked the students to write answers to these questions: If you had been a money changer, how would you have felt and why? If you had been there as a disciple, how would you have felt and what would you have thought? After writing their attitudes from two different viewpoints, the students were then helped to think in terms of today: What are some of the religious practices of Christians today? How do we do these things in the wrong way? What might we do?

A church school superintendent received a letter from a teacher who was sent by her church to a summer leadership school. During the week the teacher wrote:

"I am overwhelmed when I try to think of what we need to do in our church. It amazes me that our kids come to church at all. If our church school closed, it wouldn't matter. Long-range plans will mean complete and honest evaluation of the entire program for boys and girls in our church school."

Had this teacher waited to express her attitudes when she reached home the superintendent might never have known them, unless he had remembered to ask her soon after her return. But writing as she did, in the full flush of enthusiasm, her honest opinions were revealed.

One's writing tells much about him, and it is a privilege for a church school teacher to know persons through their thoughts expressed on paper. A vacation church school teacher attempted to get acquainted with a new group of junior children through the use of writing. She asked them the first morning to write at the top of their papers the words, "I am." Then they were to list ten things about themselves.

Elisabeth wrote:
I am a girl,
a Girl Scout,
a fast runner,

Bobby wrote:
I am super smart,
in the fourth grade,
live in Queens,

going into the fourth grade,
a little smart,
swimmer,
reader,
a sister,
horse lover,
table setter.

have a dog,
am 7¾ years old,
good in behavior,
skipped the second grade,
an excellent swimmer,
five inches tall,
a millionaire.

As the children wrote they laughed and joked, then shared their papers. Later, when the junior department staff evaluated the session, they took time to think about each child. They wondered how Bobby would get along with the older fifth- and sixth-graders inasmuch as he was so young. They caught his sense of humor in the last two items and his self-satisfaction in the adjectives "smart, good, and excellent." They noted that he mentioned his dog but not his baby brother. They looked forward to getting better acquainted with him.

Writing Reveals Inner Thoughts

A more unusual use of writing is for the purpose of releasing the hidden thoughts and fears of children. A second-grade teacher showed her class a Christmas card that she had received, *Mother and Child* as painted by a Vietnamese. She did not call it a Christmas card or interpret it to the children. She said simply: "This is a mother in Vietnam. What is she thinking? How does she feel as she holds her baby? Write what you think about her." Three of the children answered in these ways:

1. "It looks like a bomb just came down and killed her husband and her name is Jane. Jane's baby's name is Dan. Dan is thinking about all the good times he had with his father to make him a little bit happier."

2. "She is frightened and she doesn't want anything to happen to her baby. She looks like somebody is going to do something to herself and her baby. She's praying to God. She wants food and she wants clothes and she wants a life and she's sad."

3. "The baby needs support and education to get smart—get it? The mother is frightened—so what? Everyone is frightened."

If seven-year-olds have such feelings, it is important to get them out in the open. Children absorb more of the adult world of conversation and news broadcasts than we may suspect. A sensitive teacher can help them with their hidden fears and unhappy thoughts. "Yes, we are all frightened some of the time but not all the time," she responded. Fear was an accepted emotion.

Young people in their late teens go through a period of self-absorption and often feel the need to pour out their inner thoughts to an understanding adult. An eighteen-year-old wrote to her camp counselor:

Dear Mrs. Smith:
    How do you try to find yourself internally, externally? I'm homely, ugly, and all that jazz. But I want to find out what I am inside—what I'd be best doing. How do you find this out?

Sara

Only an understanding camp counselor would receive a letter like that. Teen-agers confide in and ask help from adults who are sincere in listening to them and believing in them as persons.

The mother of an eighteen-year-old was interested in learning some of the deeper thoughts of her son as situations made it possible. He had been asked to give the pastoral prayer in morning worship on Youth Sunday when the young people would lead the entire service. He worked on it all week—writing, deleting, adding. She was amazed at the depth of concerns that her boy expressed in his prayer that Sunday morning.

A high school senior who plays a guitar and enjoys folk songs began to pour out her own thoughts one night after youth fellowship meeting. It had been a flop. The leadership was poor, the attendance was the worst yet. As a few of the girls sat around afterward, she picked up her guitar and sang:

Youth today, yes, you and I,
We need God's love.
We need our hate lifted;
To be enlightened from above.

"Oh, God is dead," they say to me,
"God is dead," they say.
"Oh, God is dead," they say to me,
And then they turn away.

Help them, help them, I beg to you,
Help them, I beg of you;
For God's not dead, oh, no—
It's this church and you.

(*Refrain*)
Look around you, look around you,
Where are our youth today?
Well, look around you, look around you
For them that you've turned away.

—*Beth Hack*

A young student away from home found a group of young adults in a city church with whom she could identify. Through this association and Bible study she began to realize what was causing some of her tension and unhappiness. So she wrote it out in a letter to God, saying she would like to tell him what a meaningful part he had played in her life recently. Here are excerpts: "My family life has lost love. . . . My father and I do not speak now. . . . I have discovered where I've been wrong. . . . My parents and I have different ideas, but they should not have to change because *I* think they should. . . . I am too independent . . . my pride . . . . God, You are LOVE and You can teach me . . . ." It helped this young woman to put her thoughts on paper, and she also wrote them to her parents and found reconciliation.

On the bulletin board of his study, a research mathematician posted a priceless reminder to himself from his eight-year-old daughter.

> Dear Daddy
>   I love you a lot. It is just
> that some times I do not like
> the way you are.
>   from
>   Debby

Her ability to express this and her knowledge that her father would accept it describes the relationship between them.

Motivation for Writing

Writing one's ideas helps a person in conceptual thinking. Individuals express themselves freely when their relations with persons are frank, concerned, and accepted. To help children open themselves in writing, a teacher must encourage the dreaming of big ideas, stimulate the spirit of inquiry, listen carefully, and accept ideas as expressed. He does not impose his ideas by correcting and revamping what the children create. He encourages them to write more and more, and to do it again in another way. He is not afraid of silence in the room as the children think. He sparks, listens, reads, approves, asks questions, praises, and shares expressive writing by reading it to the class. The reaction of youth to the hearing of Ps. 12 without knowing it is a psalm, simply a poem, is to identify with a contemporary who writes of current times.

Creative writing is sometimes hard to get. In a culture in which conformity is expected in education and religion, boys and girls try to talk and write alike. They are rewarded for conformity by good grades, nods of approval, and smiles. The "loner" gets a frown and sometimes correction and rejection. For example, what should be our reaction to the answers given on the written test about the picture study of *The Adoration of the Shepherds?* Should we correct the boy who wrote, "Everyone is looking at the kid"? Others in the class replied to this question: "Because Christ is the center" and "Because Christ is the Son of God." The latter answers conform. When only typical answers are acceptable, the spirit and uniqueness of a child are dulled. Combinations of words can be trite and acceptable, or new and startling.

One may wonder how the church school teacher felt who received this message in a hand-painted birthday card from an eighth-grader:

> From a jerky Christian
> to a great one,
> HAPPY BIRTHDAY!
> Your artist,
> Mary

A teacher of sixth-graders stimulated them to do creative writing in this way. One Palm Sunday she helped them think about Jesus' triumphal entry by reading a story of how it might have felt to have been in Jerusalem that day. The story was written in the first person from the viewpoint of a teen-age boy. Added to the Biblical record were such personal observations as: how warm it was that day, how excited the crowd became in shouting and waving palm branches, how puzzling it was that this procession did not look like that of a real king with soldiers. The concluding sentence was: "As I stood watching I decided that Jesus really must be the man my grandfather told me would come someday—the man we would call our Messiah."

After reading the story the teacher asked the children what it was the writer had said that made them feel he was really there. They analyzed his method. She suggested: "You, too, can pretend that you lived in Palestine when Jesus was there. Here are some Bible references that tell about several important events. After you read one, pretend that you were there and tell in your own words what happened. Each story can be the chapter of a book and I will write your chapters here on these large pages fastened to the wall."

She handed out 4″ x 6″ index cards with a reference from Mark written on each one. For about ten minutes they read silently, then wrote the story as if they had been there when the event occurred. As each spoke, the teacher wrote the story quickly with a Magic Marker on a large page. The children discovered that together the chapters formed a brief survey of the life of Jesus. Next she asked the children to illustrate their chapters with pictures. Colored papers, crayons, and Magic Markers were already on the tables so the children eagerly set to work.

The first chapter (Mark 1:9-15) began, "I saw Jesus baptized by John at the Jordan River." In her illustration the girl depicted v. 10 when Jesus came up out of the water: "He saw the heavens opened and the Spirit descending like a dove." Other chapters were: Jesus calling Levi, healing on the Sabbath, replying to the request to sit on his right hand in the future Kingdom, Jesus before Pilate, the crucifixion, and the burial.

The boy who had the last chapter (Mark 15:42-47) wrote: "A member of our council named Joseph got enough courage and went to Pilate and asked for the body of Jesus. Then he bought a shroud from my shop and wrapped it around Jesus' body and placed him is a cave."

Interest during the entire session was keen. The teacher had challenged the children's thinking by asking them to read the Bible from a new point of view. Next she inspired them to creative writing, and finally, to creative art expression. Her leisurely schedule allowed sufficient time for each part of the work. She kept quiet or answered individual questions in low tones as needed so that the children were truly free to do their own study and expression.

In another church during Lent the junior high teacher worked with the junior and senior high teachers in coordinated study that would lead to expression in a family service on Good Friday afternoon. The work of the juniors in role-playing for that service was described in Chapter 7 with their three vignettes: Why Did Jesus Have to Die? The junior high teacher led his class in Bible exegesis on the same Scripture passages and every Sunday helped them to deduce contemporary counterparts for the religious leaders who feared Jesus and the disciples who followed him. On Palm Sunday he gave out paper, pencils, and Magic Markers saying: "We have been studying the events and teachings in Jesus' life that led up to Good Friday. Today let's respond to what we have discovered. Do anything you want in drawing or writing." Katie Driver expressed herself this way for Good Friday:

He died, serving.
Living, he was a lonely leader.
And for what? Did the priests want
   to defend their faith? Or did
   the people just not understand
   what he had to say? Do we
   still understand?
Today we are here to mourn his
   death in Golgotha, Memphis, Jerusalem,
   Saigon, Hiroshima, New York, Chicago

During the week after Easter each child in the third and fourth grades received five small pictures through the mail from their church school teachers. A brief note said: "What do these pictures mean to you? Bring them next Sunday and we'll discuss them." The teaching team was using a different device for reviewing the meaning of Easter. They sent these pictures:[19]

Washing the Feet of the Disciples	Ford Madox Brown
The Last Supper	Da Vinci
Agony in the Garden	El Greco
The Crucifixion	Rubens
Resurrection of Christ	Bellini

That Sunday the juniors were given five Bible references to look up and match one to each picture. Then they chose to do different types of expressional activity. One was to write the Bible passages in their own words. Each "modern translation" had the unique freshness of a child, such as this on the Last Supper.

All the disciples had got together for Passover, though nowadays we call it the Last Supper, because it was! But little did they know that it would be the last meal Jesus would have for a long time.

As they ate, he broke bread and he said, "Take this bread, it is my body. Eat it in good will."

And as they drank he said, "Take the cup. This is my blood. Drink it and be happy."

Passover is a Jewish holiday. In it they celebrate being freed from being slaves in Egypt. Then, as you must suppose, Jesus was a Jew. Well, you are right.

The Bible rewrites were mimeographed so each child could use them with his pictures to make his own book of *The Easter Story*.

The last decade has not only produced several new translations of the Bible but also religious folk songs, blank verse, poetry, litanies, and prayers in modern idiom. God's truth needs to be expressed in new ways and today's children and youth should be encouraged to do so. Printing original work in the church bulletin, newsletter, or a special yearly booklet encourages creative writing; young writers enjoy seeing their written words in print.

Words, written words—always old, yet ever new as each growing person finds them and builds his meanings of life, thinking God's thoughts after him.

9
Learners Need to Talk

When David announced one day that his father was going on a ship to Germany the four-year-olds had an excited discussion.

"Germans are bad," said Tsutomo.

"Germans are bad. Americans are good," said Andrew.

"Why?" the teacher asked.

"Because they had a war," said the first boy.

"My uncle was in a war and a German shot him," said the second.

"The reason is because the United States was fighting against the Germans in the war. And there was a war with Japan," said Michael.

Tsutomo added, "Wars are going on now."

"Yes, there are wars in some countries right now," the teacher replied. "Are all Germans bad? How can you tell? Do you know any German people?" She asked one question at a time for thinking.

"I know some Germans who are my neighbors. They're good," said Donald.

"Germans are bad. Americans are good," reiterated Andrew.

"Are all Germans bad?" the teacher asked again.

"No," said Fred, "only some of them."

"Are all Americans good?" the teacher repeated.

Silence. Then David spoke up and said: "No, you see there was a church. It was a Negro church. All Negroes were in it. So some people came along and threw a bomb in the window."

"Was this in America?"

"Yes."

His story was effective.

"Some Americans are bad," a child decided.

"Yeh, some Americans are bad," chorused other children.

These children were working on a big idea and making generaliza-
tions on the basis of what they knew, namely, what they had heard
adults say. The teacher tried to help them ferret out the adult stories
that led to prejudice and discover the truth about people, the goodness
and the badness in all nations. She might readily have told them that
Andrew was wrong about Germans being bad and Americans, good.
Instead, they probed and found it out themselves.

The teacher was particularly interested in David's contribution that
day. Usually he did not talk much, but on this day he stood up, walked
over to the teacher, and in great earnestness told his story. It was
evident that he had been impressed with family conversation of current
news.

Learning Words for Talking

One has only to watch and listen to a jabbering toddler to discover
the joy of talking. His sounds do not make sense yet, but when coupled
with actions he usually makes himself understood. Gradually his parents
urge him on with: "Say bye-bye" and "Say thank you." They are so
eager to have their child communicate with them verbally that they
talk with him so he can hear their clearly spoken words. Amazingly it
comes and then he seems to talk incessantly.

A nursery teacher is used to hearing children talk for the pleasure
of talking. She needs patience to give honest, uncluttered answers when
children ask questions—who, what, when, where, why, and how. She
recognizes their need for companionship in some of their sociable
chattering. They not only need freedom to talk but also an adult who
listens and hears what they say. A child arrives at church school. The
teacher can ignore him because of her interest in his parent. Or she
may talk with him first and then to the parent. The conversation gives
him a sense of personal worth. The relationship between the two is not
that of teacher and pupil so much as that of two friends talking together.
A rapport between them is gradually built week by week because each
cares about the other and listens when he speaks. Even without saying
the words, a young child's whole being reflects the spirit and desire
of "Let *me* say it!"

Two boys and a girl, all three years old, sat at a table using crayons.
One boy said to the other: "I wike you. You wike she?" The second
did not understand but caught on after it was repeated, and he replied:

"Yes, I like you. And I like her too. But I am making a picture for my mommy." The listening teacher was glad that the child who could not yet form the sound of *l* was understood by the other boy and accepted in conversation.

There are some occasions in the church when children under six ask questions and receive strange answers. Recently a mother and her three-year-old walked through the sanctuary on the way to his church school room. The table was spread for celebrating the Lord's Supper. It was Edward's first time to see a table with white linens in the chancel. "What's that? What is it for?" His mother was caught off guard and explained, "Jesus and his friends are going to have a party." "When? I want to see them." As she tugged on his hand to urge him along toward his room he stopped and said, "But, Mommy, I want to see Jesus." The mother was quite upset by the time she got to the three-year-olds room and talked it over with a perceptive teacher who helped her analyze her reply. "Do you honestly believe that the Sacrament is what you described to Edward? If so, your words are symbolic and not understood by a young child. Would it be more honest to say that the Lord's Supper is a time when people of the church remember an event in Jesus' life? And go on from there according to Edward's responses?"

In a kindergarten room a five-year-old said, "God and Jesus are the same." "Oh, no, they aren't!" replied a teacher. Another teacher, overhearing the conversation said, "I'll talk with you about that later, Stevie." She forgot it in class but talked with his mother to inquire if they had been discussing the Trinity at home. The mother knew nothing of where he had acquired this idea. But a neighbor reported that when Stevie rode home from church he said to those in the car: "I'm having a hard time with my teachers. They don't know God and Jesus are the same." This was a challenge to the two teachers, the mother, and the neighbor. They made an appointment with the minister to discuss the Trinity for their own understanding and for interpretation to young Stevie. They agreed that the teacher's first approach should be acknowledging to Stevie that she had forgotten her promise and then asking him what he knows about God and Jesus being the same. Simply agreeing with him might be sufficient for the time, it would depend on what he explained and asked.

For a young child a verbal relationship to an adult is very important. There are several reasons for his talking:

1. For the sheer pleasure of hearing himself and others.

2. For companionship—"I like your beads," "You have gold in your mouth" (when a filling was spotted!).

3. To get attention, showing off his vocabulary even though he may not understand the words he uses, such as "hate," "overloaded wires," "pteradactyl."

4. To get information by asking the who, what, when, where, why, and how questions.

5. And after talking he learns to become a responsible listener.

Busy adults sometimes ignore young children, but teachers eager to build meaningful relationships concentrate on conversing with them:

1. By *listening* and replying as necessary.

2. With *genuine interest* in the person as a friend, not using trite and halfhearted replies.

3. By *asking:* What do *you* mean? What does *that* mean?

4. By *answering* in terms the person can understand, by *asking* him thought-provoking questions to help him find his answer, or by *admitting* that one does not know but together they could look for the answer.

5. By *expecting* one person to listen to another.

At first glance these reasons for seeking a verbal relationship and the teacher's methods of sustaining it may seem to apply only to children under six who are very subjective. But test it. Think of a ten-year-old, a teen-ager, an adult. In different degrees it applies to them, too, along with their ability to be objective in thinking and speaking.

Teachers Encourage Oral Expression

It is usually the leader of a group who must build rapport and understanding. His conversations with individuals about their pastimes, interests, and concerns will foster the same between class members. Basically it is what the song expresses, "Getting to know you." Then the group becomes a place where a person can say what he thinks and be heard and still be secure in friendships. This makes learning more possible and pleasurable. Within such an atmosphere speaking informally will be encouraged for several reasons.

In a leadership training class the leader wanted to find out how much the teachers knew about the learning process. He wanted information about their backgrounds. So he asked them to recall their own learning experiences. "Think of something you have learned recently. How did you learn it?" There was a lively sharing of sports, cooking, and teaching methods. One woman reported that she had gone to a demonstration-teaching class and had learned new ways of observing

children in order to understand their reactions. After class she confided to the leader: "I went to that demonstration class five months ago, but this is the first time anyone has asked me to tell what I learned." By the excitement in her voice it was evident that she took pride in saying something to others that was meaningful to her.

A new teacher in a primary department began the Christmas session by asking the children, "What is Christmas all about?" They made a list on the chalkboard. From it she could see how much they understood about the incarnation and how important it was to them in relation to Santa Claus and toys. Another primary teacher arranged a bulletin board of pictures on the life of Jesus with this question: "The people of the early church told others about Jesus. Would you be able to tell these stories?" The children accepted it as an opportunity to tell one another what they knew.

When a group of three-year-olds in church school were learning to use the blocks in class, one child hastily reached out and pulled many blocks to his corner for himself. The teacher said: "We need to learn to share. Sharing is a happy thing. Does anyone know what it means?" Philip replied, "It's not stealing everything so nobody has any." Whether or not the offender learned anything that day about sharing blocks is unknown, but the probability is strong that he did because another child told him so clearly. Children often learn more quickly from one another than from a teacher.

Besides finding out what a group know by asking them questions, the leader also helps them to fix it in their minds or memories. This is a second reason for encouraging individuals to speak. The saying of the Lord's Prayer every Sunday has fixed it in the minds of persons without a deliberate effort to memorize it. An expectant mother tells of her two-and-one-half-year-old saying something repeatedly as if to help herself remember it. When she had sucked the bath water from a washcloth her mother said, "Beth, this is something you will have to teach our new baby—not to drink the bath water." Little Beth went around for two weeks saying, "Teach baby, not to drink the bath water" over and over again.

Adults know that it is good to remember pleasant happenings and teachers can guide children in oral expression for this purpose. As one way in which they might express their concern for a larger number of children than their own, a church decided to take its vacation school to vacant lots instead of holding it within church walls. Teams composed of adults, teen-agers, and college students studied together and worked out plans so that one team would work mornings and another work afternoons in different vacant lots of the ghetto area.

Just before the starting date of this vacation church school a bombing and riot took place. The area was still policed by helmeted marines when the vacation school teams began work. At a vacant lot the team called for children to come to playtime. Shouts of fun reverberated down the street as more and more gathered to play games and sing together. People looked out of tenement windows for the source of the new and different sounds outdoors. They saw children listening to stories, looking at pictures, and enjoying ice cream. At the close the minister, who was leader of one team, talked with the crowd of children and asked: "What are you thankful for? Who would like to come over here and tell the rest of us what you are thankful for?" The response was immediate. In their spontaneous way, individual children spoke of "the blue sky," "my family," "ice cream," and other things. By letting the children speak of the good things in their lives, their thoughts were turned from possible bitterness to joy and gratitude. In a small way these leaders had helped children to know that there are people who care about what happens to them and will listen to them speak. And when they spoke, other boys and girls heard what they said too.

A third reason for getting persons to "say it" is that when a person takes part in group discussion he becomes a part of that group. He is no longer looking on from the sidelines. He makes a contribution and has a stake in what is going on. His idea may be rejected by the group, in which case he is further involved in supporting or altering his idea. Or if the statement is accepted and used to further group thinking, then he is still part of the process as well. When he leaves that class or meeting he will remember best his own participation. This is why a good leader tries to get every individual to speak in the group or take part in a subgroup such as a buzz session of two or three.

In the fourth place, when we speak our thoughts we share opinions. If a young person sits mute in a class, there is no way of knowing his opinion or of helping him to grow and enlarge. Opinions are usually based on emotional reaction or past experience. They are not necessarily true and justifiable. In a group discussion opinions are reacted to by other persons. They are traced to their source: "Why do you feel that way?" They are weighed for accuracy: "Your idea would not always be so. For example, what about this case?" They are reinforced:

"You're right. I agree with you because . . . ." Reflection later adds to one's thinking of what he said.

In a junior class there hangs a poster of beautiful colors with a quotation from Dag Hammarskjöld: "For all that has been—thanks, For all that will be—yes." After the group had studied "Whatsoever things are true . . ." (Phil. 4:8) and "Lay not up for yourselves treasures . . ." (Matt. 6:19–29), they tried to apply Jesus' teachings to their own lives. As they progressed the teacher looked at the poster and asked, "What do you suppose this means?" They were quiet for a while, then one child said, "It's quite clear to me that no matter what happened to Dag Hammarskjöld he was thankful. Whether good or bad he knew it had meaning." Another added: "In looking back he could be thankful so he learned that in looking ahead he could accept what might happen and be thankful." Having an opportunity to speak helped these children to interpret Biblical passages and to learn from another Christian who worked hard at living for the benefit of others.

A younger group of juniors has found that *Good News for Modern Man,* The New Testament in Today's English Version, is most helpful in their Bible study. The teacher wondered why they liked it. He brought a tape recorder to class and established a situation: How would you tell other people about this book, *Good News for Modern Man?* They spoke individually then played back the tape so they could hear what each had said. "O.K., folks, here we are and now for the book of the week. It is the new Bible made by the American Bible Society. It is called *Good News for Modern Man.* Get one soon." "Hello! I'm your happy book dealer and I'm here to give you some nice books. I have the New Testament—it's great. Everybody come buy. It's a rush sale." It was evident that when the children stood up to speak they thought in terms of selling but only on a commercial basis, not on what the book meant to them.

Fifth and last, when verbal expression is encouraged the teacher often gets some evaluation of his teaching. After a primary teacher had told the story of the stoning of Stephen she asked questions. "What was Stephen doing when the crowd rushed upon him? What did he do when they stoned him?" Alice replied: "The men threw stones at Stephen because he kept talking about Jesus and God. They didn't like what he was saying." Shauna said, "Stephen prayed when they hurt him and asked God to excuse them for what they were doing." One does not truly understand something until he can explain it, describe it, or interpret it in his own words. Not what does "it" mean, but rather, what do "you" mean? *Say* it!

Frustration and Controversy

A child in a group of adults was so frustrated at not being able to talk that when he finally found an opening he asked, "May I say something?" Some boys and girls give up rather than persist and feel that what they want to say is probably not important anyway. One tension is built on top of another if the first is not released. Sometimes a kindergarten teacher will have a typewriter in the room and whenever a child wants to "say something" he knows that he can tell it to her and she will type it for him. When she reads it to him they talk about it. This helps him analyze why he feels as he does.

It is a basic human need to communicate with other persons. Sometimes "let me say it" really means "let me let off steam," let me release frustration and pent-up emotions. Fortunate is the young child who is heard by a concerned teacher or parent. Fortunate, too, is the youth or adult who is encouraged to "say it" and keep on saying it until he is relieved rather than being told to "be quiet and keep still." Sometimes a person is tense when in a church group and it is essential that he be heard out. This does not mean that a teacher gives his entire attention and time to one individual and excludes the others. For the entire group learns to listen and to respond—to one another, thereby helping one another.

A staff of junior teachers decided not to have church school classes on Easter Sunday but to encourage their children to attend the morning service of worship with their families. On the following Sunday they discussed what had happened in that service. For the most part the children liked the music, especially the Hallelujah Chorus. As for the rest, one boy said, "I was bored." No one pounced on him, just listened to what he said. Another asked: "Do you really mean Jesus is alive? I'd like to meet him," and no one laughed.

Such an atmosphere of frankness is needed for adults in the church too. We refer to someone as being biased or opinionated and we mean he is deep in a rut where he will not listen or try to change. The truth of the matter is that he has no place to meet differing opinions in a climate that permits free speaking, in a place where he is valued despite differences. Where else but the church is an appropriate place for such learning? Even controversial discussions are acceptable. Where a person feels secure and can express himself, he begins to listen to others, and he gradually drops off the old and takes on the new. Adults cannot possibly teach if they are rejected by others as biased persons. Some churches nowadays are planning their annual meetings around controversial issues instead of yearlong reports. Members are alerted to the issues ahead of time so they will be ready for the discussion. Someone has said: "What have you to fear in change and controversy, O Christian? You, who have been born anew in Christ."

Teachers, Too, Need to Talk

There is an important angle in oral expression from the standpoint of a teacher too. He knows what he believes from studying the life and teachings of Jesus and from having experiences with God through

Jesus Christ. He wants to share with others that which he cherishes. Some things he must say—say them directly and convincingly. In the act of saying, his own life is shared and those who hear are affected.

Another time when the teacher must "say it" is when he wants to give the experience of someone else. If he teaches children, this may take place in the form of a story—a story that he relives as he tells it to boys and girls. A teacher of youth or adults may give another's experience through an incident from biography, a newspaper incident, or even a television interview he has heard. All of these add to the thinking of the group, and he must "say it" as well as help pupils to "say it."

10
Books Are for Reading

A group of Idaho young people had made arrangements to take part in a work camp in northern Oregon. As they were studying the map, planning their transportation and route, the leader caught a glimpse of Waiilatpu about twenty-five miles out of their way. She asked if anyone had been there. No one had. "Does anyone know who Marcus and Narcissa Whitman were?" "Missionaries." "Why would a national monument be erected to them?" The result of this conversation was an eager search for books about the Whitmans, a decision to go to Waiilatpu en route, and much discussion of the issues the Whitmans faced as Christian missionaries.

Reading the written page is a major source for knowledge about persons and nations of the past and also a means of current communication. We can read about colleagues half a world away who are engaged in the same research as our own, in similar governmental problems, in like theological probings, and in expressing the meaning of life in drama, novel, poetry, and biography. Persons find great satisfaction in having information and using it. Information leads to concepts and concepts give meaning to life. Reading is an excellent way to gain information about oneself and the world, and a vital way to gain knowledge of God and his mighty acts in history. To be involved in reading is essential in church education and it is well coupled with sensory learning and expressional activity.

What Happens in Reading?

One can hardly imagine a church or church school where no reading is done. Scripture, responsive readings, prayers, hymns, and creeds

are all read. Yet there is no guarantee of learning in the act of reading. It is what happens to the person when he reads that matters, what goes on in his mind and heart as meanings of words give him directions, ideas, ideals, concerns. Ask yourself, for instance: "What did that psalm say to me last Sunday in the morning service of worship when I read the responsive reading? Did any phrase of the hymn apply to me? Why did that printed prayer of confession read in unison bring a lump into my throat?"

A church school teacher thinks of his own class and asks: Does my group read? What do individual members read? How do they use what they read? What happens to them because they read?

Methods used in connection with reading are almost as important as the reading itself. Methods can set the stage and help determine the attitudes of the class toward reading matter. A teacher can make books enticing and meaningful.

Certainly the Bible did not speak to children clearly in the Sundays of the past when it was read aloud, one verse per pupil around the class. This method was often used to initiate the session by reading the Scriptural text. But poor readers fumbled, good readers excelled, and the Biblical content was disjointed.

The writer well remembers the church school class she attended when she was a junior in high school. The teacher read, but members of the class did not read. That teacher was an expert lecturer and she made her subject seem important. She must have read volumes every week in preparing her lesson. In class we were expected to read silently while the teacher read the Scripture aloud—that is, we read if we had brought our Bibles. On occasion I have had a slightly guilty feeling for not remembering all that history of Judah and Israel to which I was exposed. I was there, but I was not involved.

Today teachers may begin with a discussion of a problem incident and help pupils search for guidance in the Bible and in other books. As a student reads, he thinks of the problem, wonders, asks questions, listens to others, and makes statements in the process of digging out values and meanings for himself. The teacher's part is not to hand out his own predigested conclusions but to challenge the pupil to read and discover truth for himself. A learner sorts out information and accepts or rejects, classifies and reclassifies such information as he needs. The key factor for a teacher to remember is that each person must do things for himself in order to be a learner. An adult knows from experience how it feels to be stimulated by the discovery of knowledge. So his job, whether parent or teacher, is to stimulate and guide others.

Books Are Meant to Be Read

In this age of photographic magazines, advertisements, pictures on packaged foods, television, and movies, children and young people are learning much without reading a word. This is particularly evident among nonreaders, the children under six, and the hoards of information they reveal. It is reported that the average eighteen-year-old today has seen twenty feature films for every book he has read. Yet adults realize the need for reading and push children as quickly as they can, which was just what William's father did.

Bill was in the third grade and could not read; parents and teachers were distressed. One day at school a teacher, walking quietly down the hall, found Bill reading a science magazine. Quickly he put it away. "Go ahead and do what you were doing," she said. "Don't mind me." Then they talked about reading and what fun it was, and about his not being able to read in class. Finally he blurted out, "If I learn how to read, I have to be a lawyer and I don't want to be a lawyer." The next day Bill's homeroom teacher invited his father for a conference. She asked him if he would be willing to give up his dream of his son becoming a lawyer for the ability of the child to read. The father hesitated. Then accepted. She did not tell him that Bill could already read, but it was not long till he found out.

Persons Motivate Reading

Adults in home, school, and church must ever be alert for ways to motivate good reading and to spark interest in the printed page as an exciting source of information. The first way to do this is to be enthusiastic about one's own reading. A teacher of adults initiated a study of the Gospel of Luke by telling the class of his experience the week before in reading Luke at one sitting. He saved details of his personal reactions to tell later and invited the members of the group to read this Gospel as he had. Then, he told them, they would share experiences in class next Sunday. This same teacher, while reading *The Source,* by James Michener,[20] could not keep it to himself. As he progressed in his reading, he talked about the book. An illustration with regard to Palestinian life during the time of the prophets fitted perfectly into class discussion one Sunday. He used a quotation from the novel at another time. Before he finished the book, a member of the class had asked to borrow it. Every group responds to the enthusiasm of its leader.

Church librarians are often a key to motivating a person or group to read. Displays of books and the librarian's knowledge about them interests readers. One librarian visits each church school department from primary up about every other month. She carries with her books for the group, some of which deal with curriculum themes currently being studied and others with reading for pure pleasure. In June she announces that baskets of books for the whole family may be taken out for vacation reading. This librarian's enthusiasm is contagious, and her know-how for promotion is always fresh and inviting.

One primary superintendent discovered parents who were interested in putting religious books on their children's own bookshelves but did not know how to select such books. She sought book lists from her own denomination and from a nearby theological seminary. She also used the Friendship Press catalog and there found *No Biscuits at All!*

by Lois Horton Young.[21] This book was so pertinent to the lives of her mobile families that she purchased two dozen copies and sold them to parents. Later *David, My Jewish Friend,* by Alice L. Goddard,[22] proved to be just as popular.

A certain amount of satisfaction and pride comes from reading a book when you know someone else who has read it and with whom you can discuss it. A certain minister who loans his personal books asks each reader to write his name on the flyleaf after he has finished it. Sometimes readers get together to discuss a book. Often they do serious study of a single book of the Bible with the minister.

One teacher of young children buys good books and loans them to her kindergarten children. She has a small suitcase in which a book or two travels every week into a different home. Each child is eager for his turn to have the suitcase and neighbors often share the book during the week.

Activities Motivate

Group projects are excellent motivations for reading. The Idaho young people who visited the Whitman National Monument, reported earlier, were fascinated by a historical novel, *To Heaven on Horseback,* by Paul Cranston.[23] Centered on Narcissa Whitman, it describes the sheltered family life she left in the East, their trip West, and their life at Waiilatpu.

A class of city children planned for a Saturday in the country. They needed to do certain reading ahead of time in order to be ready for their experiences at a large dairy farm, an orchard, and a limestone quarry. Anticipation along with some knowledge prepared them for keener observation. Similar preparation is needed when a rural group goes to a city museum to see certain pieces of art. Children will search ambitiously in books and magazines if they are motivated to do so ahead of time.

More than once the decision to do dramatization has forced a high school class into eager and careful Bible-reading. One Lenten season a class decided to act out the trial of Jesus. They chose lawyers, judge, and jury. But in order to know what the accusations were and what the defense could be, they had to reread the Gospels, use the concordance to find certain incidents, and read the exegesis in *The Interpreter's Bible* for an explanation of words and customs.

A young adult group had a theater party to see the play *J. B.*, by Archibald MacLeish. They returned home fired with determination to study The Book of Job, which was used as a vehicle for the play. Later they discovered that similar study was necessary to check authenticity of Biblical movies; that something happens to the Bible story when used in Hollywood productions.

A writing project for adults proved to be a daily reading incentive for a sixth-grade boy. One January the ministers of a large church presented themes and Scripture passages for a Lenten devotional booklet and asked adults to write the book. Each person or couple wrote only one message. Parents of an eleven-year-old boy who had recently balked at attending church school were heartened by the fact that he was keenly interested in this booklet. Each day he reminded his family of worship, was eager to see who had written the message, and he did the reading aloud.

In New Jersey there is a church that has an arrangement with the public library for the loan of books during Lent. The librarian helps the church committee select books for all ages on the life of Christ. Picture books, biography, music, drama, books on great works of art, and illustrated Gospels are all included. A volunteer at the church assumes responsibility as librarian, and the rules for loaning are the same as those at the public library. This church has become an outlet of good books for special reading.

What Books Are Needed in Church Education?

Many kinds of reading are possible in church groups, but there are some key tools that ought to be available to teachers and to class members of junior age and older. Denominational plans for church libraries offer thorough lists of approved texts. Basically these include several versions of the Bible, the newest of which is *Good News for Modern Man*, The New Testament in Today's English Version. This book prints the stories and teachings by paragraphs with a title for each and line drawings as illustrations. A second-grade boy has become an avid reader and has purchased his own copy of it. Different modern translations bring new insights and recent Biblical scholarship.

Resource books are a Bible dictionary, a concordance, an atlas with century charts as well as maps, a commentary, a theology word book, and study guides. Some of these resources are printed in editions for children such as a dictionary, atlas, and encyclopedia, all of which are profusely illustrated. Denominational hymnals reflect their respective theology in the words of songs and hymns. And denominations also recommend basic books in education for in-service training as church leaders carry on their tasks.

Books that deal with Biblical truths are not to be forgotten. These include the carefully written picture books for the youngest. Two-year-old Daniel insists at church school and home: "Me read! Me do it myself!" He turns a page and pats it, talks with a vocabulary that only his parents understand, and is radiantly happy with a book. Biography, books on people of other lands, and teen-age novels can all be found based on Biblical truths.

Reading and using interesting books at church fosters reading at home. One class agreed that each boy and girl would read a book a month. As a result, the caliber of group discussion was heightened and the enthusiasm of the class grew.

To Read and to Know

Karl Barth has often been quoted as saying that a Christian should read with the Bible in one hand and the daily newspaper in the other—

reading one to understand the other. When leaders in church education do this and find the relevancy of the Word for today they become eager to communicate to others. But their communication is not so much in telling as in guiding persons—young and old—to do the same; to read, to study, to know God through Jesus Christ.

11

Living the Christian
Faith While Learning

"I'm here because I care what happens to the Negroes of Alabama. When they're whipped it hurts me. When they're clubbed I suffer. My business in life is not to be pretty. My business in life is not to make money. My business is people. I care what happens." These were the words of a young adult, with white skin, who went to Selma, Alabama, in 1965 to express her beliefs.

What does it mean to live as a Christian today? in a particular nation and place? in this particular segment of time? Around the world young and old can be seen in daring action because they are impelled by their faith in God through Jesus Christ. In some instances they have been called disloyal to their countries. But in their inmost thoughts their loyalty is to God on behalf of their fellowman in country or world. Biological warfare, water and air pollution, demonstrations, Black Power, situation ethics, coexistence—these words and phrases bring to mind the names and faces of countless courageous persons.

Despite the belief of some people, Christianity actually is not confined to patent answers, creeds, hymns, or even to membership in a respectable church. Christianity is a way of living; the way shown to man by the Son of God. The early church taught its faith before anything of Jesus' life and teachings that they could read and study was written down. From living with him, or knowing others who had seen and heard him, early Christians carried their faith in their memories and primarily in their actions and words. The relationships that existed between persons in the early Christian communities reflected something new and different to those who observed.

Young children, two and under, learn Christianity from those who care for them in much the same way. They learn through relationships and senses—through feeling tones as they are handled and through the sounds of voices. They learn basic attitudes before any meanings come through words. Even when some words are added at ages three, four, and five a child's basic understanding of Christianity comes to him through relationships. Great emphasis is placed on early experiences by an Englishman who wrote *Your Growing Child and Religion*.[24] His concern is with *religious development* in the first seven years of life so that the mind of a child will be able to absorb *religious instruction* later. At the risk of oversimplifying the complex process of laying a "religious foundation" he has written a highly stimulating book for laymen. He wants to reach persons who are "responsible for bringing children up in religion."

Many adults come in contact with children in shopping centers, church, street, school; children learn many ways and mannerisms from them. But parents and teachers, in particular, realize that they are models for children, whether they like it or not. They build the relationships of acceptance, trust, and responsibility or just the opposite. They set the patterns and values from which children will choose their own life-styles. They can be sustained by God's guidance and forgiveness. They may seek new opportunities for witness, or living in gratitude to God, for themselves and for the children in their care. Every week brings possibilities and sometimes several at once. But it takes awareness—searching out, jumping at the chance, figuring out a way, daring to do it—to help young Christians discover ways to live their faith that are genuine and not superficial.

Being Christian by Bits and Pieces

Psychology, education, sociology, theology, and medicine all contribute to the general knowledge of how growth takes place in human beings. It is not like a well-constructed stairway leading to heights in orderly fashion. It is more like the fluidity of the ocean; constant movement of the tide forward and backward with periods of calm and storm. Growth seems to come in bits and pieces that add to a person's framework of Christian concepts and his ability to live out his ideal. One such bit came in a family when the three-year-old sister asked her six-year-old brother, "How is school different from Sunday school?" He replied: "In Sunday school they want you and are glad to see you. And the teacher doesn't wear a mad face."

After church school an eight-year-old boy preceded his mother into the toddler room to get his one-year-old brother. He walked up immediately to hug the youngster as he asked the teacher: "Was Scott a good boy? Did he cry?" It was obvious that Scott's brother, as well as his parents, cared about him. From them all, including his first "teacher," Scott grows slowly into a sense of personal worth.

The plain-looking woman knew that Carrie liked her because she was forever hanging on to her. She just figured that perhaps Carrie needed more attention, or more love, or more something. But Carrie said to her one Sunday, "How did you get the way you are?" Apparently Carrie was sorting out the adults she knew and was beginning to value some more than others.

Learning by bits and pieces is true for youth and adults as well. Many want to show gratitude to God by loving his people but do not know how to go about it outside of their own small circle. Many abhor white racism and the implications of the *Report of the National Advisory Commission on Civil Disorders*. They also abhor paternalism and pushing in where they are not wanted. Thinking the issue through with persons in an organization of mixed races in their community will guide them in building friendships and in working alongside people who seem different because they are not known. Business, peace, and political groups may offer opportunities also. Sometimes young people get adults started in such relationships. The reverse is also true: adults must motivate young people and children.

Another way that has helped some youth and adults get into action is an informal group called FISH. There are about one hundred independent FISH (symbol of early Christians) groups in America copied from the original in Old Headington, England. One such group has forty members, both Catholic and Protestant, who agree to be on duty for one twenty-four-hour period a month to help people with a variety of needs ranging from companionship for the elderly, reading to the blind, making dinner for the sick, to caring for children in an emergency. The availability of help from FISH is made known through local newspapers and churches, with one or two phone numbers always ready to receive needs.

Adults who look for such ways of expressing Christian love become more aware of different potentials within themselves. Modern life tends to dull senses, inhibit creativity, and prevent genuine communication. But finding bits and pieces of rich experiences makes for Christian learning and living.

Live and Let Live

For parents it is one thing to do something yourself and another to let your children do it. When a minister was being interviewed for a new position he commented to the committee: "I think you should know something else about me. I will challenge your boys and girls to consider church occupations. For some that would mean service in other parts of the world. I cannot help speaking of such to your children, as well as to my own son and daughter."

The idea of *"let* me do it" came in a different way to the worried mother of six-year-old Phoebe who was late getting home from school. When she came Phoebe explained that she had stopped at a friend's house because her favorite doll had been broken. Still tense, the mother asked: "Why did you stop and stay so long? It wasn't your doll. Besides,

there was nothing you could do about it." With satisfaction in her eyes Phoebe replied: "I know. But, Mommy, I could help her cry!" Her mother saw in an instant the sensitive concern of her child for a friend.

Sometimes adults set the stage for a younger person's natural desire to "do it myself." A woman living in a town of many cultural backgrounds sparked interest in an International Party for children and their mothers. It was advertised in the area newspaper and by posters in store windows. The committee planned for songs, handwork, games, and dances from each country represented. Refreshments for mothers in a different room of the church promoted adult friendship too. In following years Jewish and Buddhist women in the town asked to help organize the party: its interracial and interfaith aspects have encouraged mutual concern in the community.

An insightful teacher has for years guided others in the church wherever she was living in planning a service of worship for children on Ash Wednesday focused on the mystery of Easter. In her new town she planned it with her minister, another clergyman, the priest, and the rector of the four houses of worship. About seventy children attended and besides worship learned the history of some of the Episcopal and Roman Catholic ritual. The rector burned a previous year's palm, mixed the ashes with water, and placed some on his forehead as he explained this symbol of the coming death of the Lord. This helped the children to understand and appreciate what some of their schoolmates were used to doing on Ash Wednesday. One of the ministers led the children in a prayer of confession by listing on a chalkboard the actions for which the children told him they were sorry. Using their own words and a response that he suggested, the prayer of confession that day was tailored to the worshipers. After the service in the sanctuary the children went to the social room where they had a "love feast" (another historical explanation) of hot cross buns and grape punch. These adults provided perceptual learning and let the children live their faith through access to other approaches.

The Protestant principal of a Friends elementary school wanted worship in the Quaker chapel every week to have meaning for the children who were not used to worshiping in silence. So she explained to the children the custom of the Friends but that each child could worship as he was accustomed to do in his own place of worship. They sat in silence. Finally David stood and spoke so low he could hardly be understood. The principal realized he was praying in Hebrew. A girl said: "I won't say my regular rosary prayer. I'll make up a prayer." Finally another girl was ready: "David gave the first prayer for the menorah. I'll give the second and third. They're both short prayers." Weekly chapel services in this way, where each honored the other's form of worship, became deeply moving throughout the year. It was so because a foresighted and sensitive principal had made it possible.

Live and let live has another aspect for church people today. Some of the younger generation find that the "good old hymns" of their parents and grandparents do not speak to them, nor does the liturgy and the way it is expressed. They find new ways of worshiping the same Almighty. Older adults frown upon their ways, but one way is not right and the other wrong—all generations must acknowledge that there are different and true ways of worship. History repeats: not too long ago it was John Wesley who was put out of the organized church of his country because he wanted a new way of worship. In studying the record of his devotion and influence one must admit that it seems as if the Holy Spirit worked through him as much as it worked through the mother church.

Inquiring and Doubting

"Do you choose to believe in God? I'm not sure I do," said a seven-year-old to her mother. The mother did not explode with dismay but accepted what the child said and replied: "I understand how you feel. I have felt that way sometimes too. But yes, I choose to believe in God because I know him from experience." She also knew that her seven-year-old was thinking, and testing, and that she had a long time to grow.

A new teacher in the kindergarten was perplexed and alarmed at what happened. Joey bit the arm of another child. The teacher-in-charge slapped him and said, "You know we don't do that in this room." She went over to the other teacher and added, "If the parents of that boy would be more patient with him, we wouldn't have this trouble." The new teacher doubted the wisdom of slapping the child and inquired, "Shouldn't we be patient too?"

When some information is withheld, it is certain to be what a child wants to know. And that is exactly what the junior teachers in a large department found out when the superintendent said to the classes,

"There are really ten commandments but we will memorize only nine because one of them is bad." Apparently the superintendent had an emotional hang-up on the subject of adultery. Regardless of the superintendent the teachers found it necessary to answer children's questions that day.

Some first- and second-graders were intensely interested in studying from The Book of The Acts about the time when the church was young and what its leaders did and said. They began to think of the leaders in their own church and wondered what they did and how they spoke about Jesus. So they interviewed the various staff members of their large church. First they formulated their questions, some of which were: What do you do in your church job? Have you ever been hurt for what you believe? How can God's Word best be made known today? They divided into pairs and with a portable tape recorder interviewed the various adults. Here they were inquiring and relating the church today with the early church. Hearing their own voices on tape was a new kind of perceptual learning, and talking with staff built personal relationships.

Induction Into the Church Family

In some churches children are welcomed and allowed to take part in services of worship whether they come with family, friend, or alone. But in others certain members complain about the space occupied by a child or a little restlessness shown. How will the young become the church without experiencing it? "Let the children come."

A mother of four young children showed in her actions and words what she expected of her youngsters. On the Sunday morning that baby Anne was to be baptized the entire family of six walked up to the baptismal font in their church sanctuary. After the service a ten-year-old boy stopped this mother in the hall and asked, "Why did Elisabeth, Debbie, and Bobby go up front with you to get the baby baptized?" The mother thoughtfully replied: "When Anne was baptized we promised to teach her of God. Her sisters and brother are responsible for Anne too. At home they teach her many things. We hope they will teach her of God's love." This mother expected certain family relationships and let the children know what she expected.

While the congregation of a crowded village church was singing the Doxology, a dozen or more children walked into the church with their teachers and sat on the floor in the center aisle. From there they could easily see the adults who were standing in front for infant baptism. After the minister baptized each baby he presented it to the congregation by stepping forward through the line of parents so all could see the child in his arms. At that time the congregation took its vow to aid that baby's parents in his spiritual nurture. When all were baptized the three-year-olds, remaining seated on the floor, sang, "Jesus Loves Me," and the kindergarten group sang, "I Like to Think of Jesus." Together they prayed a poem prayer, and on the following hymn left for their departments. In this same church it was understood and expected that a child would come into the morning service of worship whenever he wanted and stay as long as he physically could stay. He was welcome for part or all of the service, alone, with family or friends. Those whose parents were not interested in the church were very often

"adopted" by other adults for worship times. Children were welcome at the celebration of the Sacrament of the Lord's Supper, the ceremony of marriage, and the worship experiences of church funerals. The adults in this congregation take seriously the many facets of life and face them realistically with their children at their sides. Death, as part of life, is occasion for Christian worship.

Hand bells are becoming more widely used in American churches and members of bell choirs attend regional and national bell-ringing conventions. Youth and adults usually take part in such choirs but even junior children can learn to use hand bells. It was in a morning service of worship in Santa Fe that a choir of high school young people added an extra dimension to corporate worship. In no sense were they on display or showing off talent. They were part of the congregation's offering of worship to God. Upon inquiry, it was learned that the pastor and the director work closely with the young people on the philosophy and theology of Christian worship. They study the principles behind the order of service, the function of musicians and minister in the service, and man's response to God in worship. Members of this bell choir take rehearsals seriously and give much time and thought to their contribution, an act of devotion.

Thus, children and youth, and even adults who are newcomers, are inducted into the church family in many ways and on many occasions. Consider also the family Advent celebration in Chapter 1 and the Lenten devotional booklet in Chapter 10 as possible ways. There are church festivals for fun and fellowship such as dinners and picnics; there are family camps where family units share study and worship with units from other churches.

An electrician's concept of induction may be a useful simile. He knows that when two wires run parallel and only one of them is charged with electricity, the second becomes charged because of its proximity to the first. He calls the first conductive current, and the parallel wire, inductive current because the electricity is induced. Adults in the church who are dependent upon the Holy Spirit may be considered the conductive current. They are guarantors who help others become inducted into the church family.

The test of Christian living is not what beliefs are spoken but how they are lived. People are seeing and hearing; they are smelling, touching, and tasting life every day. But when they are aware of their senses and the keen learning that *can* come through them they are more apt to open themselves for it; to ask, seek, try, discover, and express newness in relationships with other persons. How teach and live? It is different for every person as he responds to God. But in the teaching-learning-worshiping fellowship of old and young the search continues and venturesome living for Christ takes place.

Notes

1. Katharine Whiteside Taylor, *Parents and Children Learn Together* (Teachers College, Columbia University, 1967), p. 95.

2. Byrla Carson, "The City, the Child, the Church," *Children's Religion,* June, 1966, p. 4.

3. Bruno Munari, *Libro Illegible* (Milan: Lucini, 1949).

4. *Lord, Come* (Advent) and *The Fire and the Wind* (Pentecost), filmstrips, 50 frames, 33 1/3 r.p.m. records, scripts, 3 study guides. Produced by and available from John and Mary Harrell, 148 York Avenue, Berkeley, Calif. 94708.

5. American Bible Society, 1865 Broadway, New York, N.Y. 10023.

6. The John Milton Society, 475 Riverside Drive, New York, N.Y. 10027.

7. The world's first art gallery for the blind was originated by Charles Stanford, Jr., at the North Carolina Museum of Art, Raleigh, North Carolina. Similar galleries have opened at the Wadsworth Atheneum in Hartford, Connecticut; Los Angeles County Museum; de Young Memorial Museum in San Francisco; and Brooklyn Museum of Art in New York; and several others are in the planning stage.

8. *Good News for Modern Man,* The New Testament in Today's English Version (American Bible Society, 1966).

9. The Geneva Press, Witherspoon Building, Philadelphia, Pa. 19107.

10. United Church Press, 1505 Race Street, Philadelphia, Pa. 19102.

11. The Seabury Press, 815 Second Avenue, New York, N.Y. 10017.

12. Covenant Life Curriculum Press, 8 North 6th Street, Richmond, Va. 23219.

13. Gregorian Institute of America, 2132 Jefferson Avenue, Toledo, Ohio.

14. Avant Garde Records, Inc., 250 West 57th Street, New York, N.Y. 10019.

15. *Golden Slumbers, A Selection of Lullabies from Near and Far,* A Caedmon Soundbook with High Fidelity record, 33 1/3 r.p.m. Word, picture, and sound. Caedmon Records, Inc. 505 Eighth Avenue, New York, N.Y. 10018.

16. Franklin D. Elmer, "World Wide Communion Gains New Meaning with Bread of the World," *International Journal of Religious Education,* September, 1962, p. 6.

17. Inquiries should be made to the Women's Association, First United Presbyterian Church, Port Jervis, N.Y. 12771. The designers of the banners are Rev. Richard Avery and Donald S. Marsh.

18. From *Songs and Hymns for Primary Children* (The Westminster Press, 1963).

19. Artex Prints, Inc., Westport, Conn. 06880.

20. James Michener, *The Source* (Random House, Inc., 1965).

21. Lois Horton Young, *No Biscuits at All!* (Friendship Press, 1966).

22. Alice L. Goddard, *David, My Jewish Friend* (Friendship Press, 1967).

23. Paul Cranston, *To Heaven on Horseback* (Julian Messner, Inc., 1952).

24. R. S. Lee, *Your Growing Child and Religion* (The Macmillan Company, 1963).

For Further Reading

On Growing and Learning

Almy, Millie, with Chittenden, Edward, and Miller, Paula, *Young Children's Thinking: Studies of Some Aspects of Piaget's Theory.* Teachers College Press, Columbia University, 1966. Gives an introductory view of Jean Piaget's findings.

Holt, John, *How Children Learn.* Pitman Publishing Corporation, 1967. Illustrates the natural style of young children's thinking; believes they do their best learning before going to school.

Lee, Roy S., *Your Growing Child and Religion.* The Macmillan Company, 1963. Interprets possible religious learnings that can come through the senses and early physical relationships. Describes the first seven years as crucial for "religious development" in order that the child's mind will absorb "religious instruction" later.

Pruyser, Paul, *A Dynamic Psychology of Religion.* Harper & Row, Publishers, Inc., 1968. Deals with perceptual and intellectual processes, thought, language, emotions, acts; with the development of the ego and its relationship to persons, things, and ideas.

On Planning to Teach

Bowman, Locke E., Jr., *Straight Talk About Teaching in Today's Church.* The Westminster Press, 1967. Serves as a practical guide for church school teachers in how to make the best use of their "hour a week," how to teach concepts, pursue questions, give data, and use new techniques.

Bruner, Jerome S., *The Process of Education* and *Toward a Theory of Instruction*. Harvard University Press, 1960 and 1966 respectively. Describe the philosophy of education that deals with basic concepts; are concerned with how children learn, how they can best be helped to learn, how they can be brought to the fullest realization of their capacities.

Day, John A., *Science, Change, and the Christian*. Abingdon Press, 1965. Surveys concisely science and the change it brings; how a Christian can live responsibly in behalf of human beings in all areas of life including science and technology.

Kallas, James, *A Layman's Introduction to Christian Thought*. The Westminster Press, 1969. Gives basic theological truths and teachings significant for intelligent action in an increasingly complex world.

Linderman, Earl W., and Herberholz, Donald W., *Developing Artistic and Perceptual Awareness*. Wm. C. Brown Company, 1964. Shows the necessity for sensory experiences and their contribution toward releasing the creative power within a person.

Lowenfeld, Viktor, and Brittain, W. L., *Creative and Mental Growth*, 4th ed. The Macmillan Company, 1964. Points up perceptual growth at each developmental stage of creative expression from age two through adolescence. Includes creative work with retarded and handicapped children.

Noyce, Gaylord B., *The Church Is Not Expendable*. The Westminster Press, 1969. Offers concrete help toward recovering "true religion" in an age of confusion.

9273-4

26

On the weekend that the missionaries visited the church, the children and young people were prepared to ask them relevant questions about the church's work overseas. The superintendent felt that the success of the project lay in acquainting people with representative articles used by the Thais. Seeing and handling these objects helped them understand the conditions of life and work in southern Asia.

In another church a woman from India visited a primary class wearing her sari. The children were glad to be allowed to feel the material, a fine silk, as well as to look at it and admire the beautiful hand-stitched designs. They were also interested in handling and feeling the smooth surface of a crane fashioned from the horn of a water buffalo.

Tactile Materials Stimulate Creativity

Sometimes the variety and texture of materials is an important aspect in doing creative work. An art teacher, who teaches senior high youth in church, once brought to class some unusual materials. The group was in the midst of an intensive study of Jesus' life and teachings. The

teacher suggested that the members make pictures of some incident or parable, using what she had brought: velvet, burlap, nubby wool, gauze, netting, straw, wood shavings, ribbon, braid, fringe, yarn, fur. The results were amazing. The materials, chosen for their texture, added varied effects in the drawings and paintings. Their work showed that the young people had thought deeply about how to portray a selected incident from Jesus' life.

An ornate sanctuary of wood carvings rich in symbolism meant much to a teacher, but he observed that his class of seventh-graders hardly noticed their church. He roused their curiosity and arranged a weekday meeting to explore the symbols. The teacher noticed that as each student went his way in the sanctuary to discover a symbol, he traced his fingers over the design. He felt of the loaves and grapes, of the winged lion and winged ox, of the fleur-de-lis on the ends of the pews. Questions and discussion led to a detailed study of Christian symbols in which the young people made symbols of clay. Perceptual learning came through their hands as well as their eyes.

On entering his classroom one Sunday a boy exclaimed, "This room says yes." Evidently his teacher had succeeded in providing an environment for much perceptual learning. She had attended state leadership events and maintained contact with other teachers she met there. They exchanged "wonder objects": she mailed tiny cones from tall redwood trees and received from her Southern friend a branch of a cotton plant with full, white tufts of cotton. Because her grandmother's Bible with brown velvet covers and gold clasp appealed to her, she took it to church school to let the children feel of it and compare it to their red or black Bibles. She taught in a rural church of northern California and tried to share with others the special things she had acquired, such as: an olive-wood dish from Jerusalem, a mother-of-pearl box from Bethlehem, men's headgear from Jericho. Her children felt of everything and wore the headgear.

Whole families can enjoy work that involves the sense of touch. One summer at Ghost Ranch, the United Presbyterian Conference Center in New Mexico, bona fide tepees had been set up for family camping. They provided an experience for living in the kind of home used by some of the Indians in that area. During camp other homes, native to that country, were to be built. Men from Navajo churches came to build hogans. They stripped bark from cedar logs, cut them to size, notched the ends, and fitted them into each other in hexagonal shape. They left seeing and touching experiences in relation to babies for this boy. So she invited the boy's mother and baby sister to visit class. The children gathered round while the teacher asked the mother what they might do to help her care for the baby. They hung up her coat and bonnet, they got a toy for her, they felt of her feet, and patted her head. Then they asked the baby's mother and brother if she could take a ride in the largest doll carriage. They moved her gently and slowly. It was a fun time for all. The teacher watched the brother as he gradually assumed importance and she hoped this day might help him in his relationship to baby sister.

The blossoming of a pink hyacinth with its fascinating scent was a major experience for five-year-olds in an inner-city church. Because they did not have many firsthand experiences with nature in their community, the teacher often provided some. When the bloom was old and drying one child asked: "But, teacher, how did it grow? What *are* roots?" The teacher did not use words. She simply let the child pull the bulb out of the earth and feel of the roots. Then they talked and wondered about the miracle of a growing hyacinth bulb.

Persons in the church cannot be free to learn their faith in many different sensory ways until their leaders are free. Teachers are the ones who provide a setting for learning, who look for the unusual meaning in the usual event, who encourage creative exploration. Let teachers not be afraid to try something new when they are exposed to it: using their bodies in pantomine, creative rhythmic movement, or even "finger painting" with one's feet. In the proper setting teachers can learn together without embarrassment because all are trying, reacting, being released to express and learn.

In both church and secular education there are many places to get human relations training, or sensitivity training as it is sometimes called. Its aim is to make persons more aware of themselves and their relationships to others through the sensory and physical expressions (seeing, hearing, touching) rather than the verbal. Such relations may be more authentic than those where words are casually spoken, between adult and child as well as adult and adult.

Let hands, ears, and eyes lead you into learning the way a young child learns. One's senses are miraculous avenues of response to God, his world, and his creatures.

a hole at the top of each hogan as a chimney and cut out one door and one window.

Then they covered the entire wooden structure with adobe. They slapped wet mud onto the logs, and it hardened as it dried in the hot sun. The Navajos invited the campers to help. Those who did found that sharing in the work, which meant getting their hands in the mud, was more instructive than merely driving past an Indian settlement on a superhighway at sixty miles per hour.

The Sense of Touch for the Deaf and Blind

It is important that church leaders know how to relate to persons of special need so that experiences may be natural and helpful. Materials of different textures appeal to sightless children. In their own schools they are taught the concepts of smooth and rough through the feeling of glass and pottery, velvet and course wool, smooth paper and sand paper, a planed board, and a piece of log. In church school classes there should be many objects and materials that can be used by blind persons for perceptual learning through touch.

The tactual sense is extremely valuable to deaf children as well and it is used in their training for poise and coordination. They usually have a poor sense of balance and rhythm so their muscles must be taught. movements that come naturally to persons who hear. One way of doing this is for the young child to stand next to a grand piano and bend over it with his body, head, and hands touching it. As a teacher plays a tune the child feels the vibrations and gradually comes to recognize simple rhythms. Later he can feel the vibrations without touching the piano and he learns to do dancing and creative movement to the vibration of the musical accompaniment. Deafness varies in degree, and sometimes there are poor hearers in our regular classes. The use of all other senses for the learning experiences of such persons is especially helpful.

Teachers Learn

In a room of four-year-olds the teacher watched a child stand in front of a picture of a mother and baby on the tackboard. The child looked and looked. Finally she leaned over and kissed the baby, then went hopping away. Later a boy came along, looked at the same picture, and hit it. This action suggested to the teacher that she should plan for more